Someone once said, "God can turn ~~water in~~ ~~something~~ ~~can't do~~ anything with your whining!" Bu~~t~~ teaches us that God *can* turn that ~~v~~ woman He intended her to beco~~me~~ even more good news—being a '~~ ~~ having fun!

Comedienne and Recording Artist,
M2O/INO Records

Can one be five-foot short (like me) and be a Big Girl? Jan tells us straight it's not our height but our chutzpah; our willingness to make strenuous choices on a daily basis. With crisp candor and Christ-compassion Jan calls us to the liberty of maturity. I have dipped in her well of wisdom on a number of occasions and I can verify Jan knows what she speaks of; she's truly a Big Girl!

— PATSY CLAIRMONT,
WOF speaker, Author of *The Shoe Box* & *The Hat Box*

If you want to become a mature Christian woman, be sure to read *Big Girls Don't Whine!* With her characteristic wisdom, wit, and down-home practicality, Jan Silvious has given us a book that is captivating and timely. Like a mirror, the author reveals the painful reality of our broken expectations and imperfect reactions. She weaves biblical truth into every chapter while providing hope-filled answers and realistic action steps.

—CAROL KENT,
President, Speak Up Speaker Services,
International Speaker and Author

This book is a gift to those of us who want to move beyond the injustices of the past and live in the glorious present of all God has for us. If you feel that you are stuck in your circumstances and can't move forward, Jan provides a door out of your pain and into freedom.

— SHEILA WALSH,
WOF Speaker, Author of *The Heartache No One Sees*

Jan Silvious's specialty is giving down-to-earth advice that is really heaven-sent.

—BETH MOORE,
Best Selling Author and Speaker

Big Girls Don't Whine is a perfect fit for all of us who long for a spiritual mentor, that mature woman in Christ who isn't afraid to shine a bright light in the shadowy corners of our hearts. Girlfriends, here she is: Jan Silvious offers a Big Girl's calming voice of reason and maturity in a world of "me, me, me" Little Girls. With common sense and uncommon honesty, Jan teaches us all how to become grown-up women of God. A wise and wonderful book!"

— LIZ CURTIS HIGGS,
best-selling author of *Bad Girls of the Bible*

When Jan Silvious speaks I always sit up and take note. Her words are always practical and filled with God-honoring truth. *Big Girls Don't Whine* reassures me that I can do all things through Christ who strengthens me. Jan Silvious is the big sister every girl needs.

—BABBIE MASON,
Award winning singer, song writer, speaker and author

With a skilled verbal paintbrush, full of emotional color and intellectual honesty, Jan Silvious creates a stunning portrait of what it looks like to be a Big Girl. And by the grace of God, with her accurate portrayal to guide us, the picture can one day become a mirror.

—NICOLE JOHNSON,
Women of Faith Dramatist, Author of
Keeping a Princess Heart in a Not-So-Fairy-Tale World

After reading Jan's book, I'd call myself a Big Girl with age-regression tendencies (i.e: I have whiny, little girl moments but rarely a whole day!). I love how Jan calls it as she sees it, making me feel like she's the Big Sis I never had. Her words are often convicting, but easy to take because they're softened with humor, respect and wisdom. This book will be a resource for me for years to come—one I'll return to often as I continue to mature in my understanding of myself, my purpose, my God and my world.

—LISA TAWN BERGREN,
best-selling author and president of Good Books & Company

Big Girls Don't Whine

*Getting on with the Great Life
God Intends*

JAN SILVIOUS

W PUBLISHING GROUP™

www.wpublishinggroup.com

A Division of Thomas Nelson, Inc.
www.ThomasNelson.com

Published by W Publishing Group, a Division of Thomas Nelson, Inc., P. O. Box 141000, Nashville, Tennessee 37214.

All Scripture quotations, unless otherwise indicated are taken from *The New American Standard Bible*, © 1960, 1977, 1995 by the Lockman Foundation.

Other Scripture references are from the following sources:
The Amplified Bible (AMP), Old Testament copyright © 1958, 1987 by the Lockman Foundation. Used by permission.

The Holy Bible, New International Version (NIV). Copyright © 1973, 1978, 1874, International Bible Society. Used by permission of Zondervan Bible Publishers.

The Message (MSG), copyright © 1993. Used by permission of NavPress Publishing Group.

The Holy Bible, New Living Translation (NLT), copyright © 1996. Used by permission of Tyndale House Publishers, Inc., Wheaton, Illinois 60189. All rights reserved.

The New King James Version (NKJV®), copyright © 1979, 1980, 1982, Thomas Nelson, Inc., Publishers.

Names in some anecdotes and stories have been changed to protect the identities of the persons involved.

ISBN 0-8499-4441-4

Printed in the United States of America
06 07 08 RRD 14

Dedication

For the Big Girls who have gone before and
have shown me the way, I thank you.
For the Big Girls in process who follow, I applaud you.
Sandi, Heather, Lauren, Rachel and Bekah,
you are my heart.

And for the men in my life who enjoy women
being Big Girls, I am grateful.
Charlie, David, Jon, Aaron, Luke and Ben, I love you!

*"While others may argue about whether the world ends with a
bang or a whimper, I just want to make sure mine doesn't end
with a whine."*

—BARBARA GORDON,
American TV producer and writer

Contents

Introduction

Finding the Treasure Within

W HEN YOU WERE A LITTLE GIRL, did you ever dream of growing up to be a big girl?

Did you want to hang around with the girls who were a grade ahead of you because their lives seemed so much more interesting than yours? Did you want to do the things they did and go the places they went? If so, then you already get the Basic Big Girl Philosophy: *Being a big girl beats being a little girl by a long shot.* No doubt you proclaimed to yourself or whoever would listen, *I am a big girl!* And your desire to be a big girl was fanned by all the neat things big girls get to do, like take trips, date, have jobs, make money, get married, have babies, or stay single, and stay up as late as they want!

The only problem is, when you are a big girl it can look really appealing to be a little girl again. After all, someone takes care of you, you don't have to think about money, you can send the little boys home when you are tired of them, you can hold a baby but don't have to change the dirty diapers, and—oh dear, oh dear— you have to go to bed early!

When the adult world gets a little stressful, there is no doubt that on some days, being a little girl surely would be more fun. It would be just so much easier to sit down and whine until someone came along and tucked you in for a nap. Being a little girl would just be so much easier.

I know many women who have opted for the whining and the nap instead of finding out what it means to really grow up. These women are Little Girls. Life is hard, and they want the easy way out. Other women, however, are willing to look life in the eye and make some Big Girl choices about it. Sure, it's harder than whining, but I can tell you that choosing to be a Big Girl is one of the most rewarding choices you will ever make.

Discovering the joy of being a Big Girl is like finding a treasure. It is rich and valuable but not always obvious. Big Girls know the joy of being grown up. They know the challenges and responsibilities are greater, but the freedom and confidence are greater too. Big Girls don't have to whine. They can say what they mean and mean what they say. Big Girls don't have to nap to get over their stress unless they just want to, and then they don't have to ask permission. They just do it. Big Girls possess strength and security and *add* to any situation or relationship, while Little Girls seem to take away from it.

Being a Big Girl is what all those years you lived as a real little girl were about. The lessons you learned, the mistakes you made, the insecurities revealed in you, all make the treasure of the Big Girl inside an incredible find. This treasure allows every Little Girl to experience the freedom God intends for her. It is the freedom to move on from the past to find healthy relationships. It is the freedom to be a confident Big Girl in a whiny Little-Girl world. It is the freedom to experience a life of potential and vision. The treasure of a Big-Girl life is available to every Little Girl.

This priceless state of being is intended by God for each woman He creates.

When you find the Big Girl inside, you find the person who feels at home in her own skin, who accepts her circumstances as the place of God's pleasure, and who has the skills to maneuver through this life with wisdom from above. You find the woman who can live life with purpose and passion. That's what this life with God is all about. We aren't here just to take up space and be miserable. We weren't created to play at recess all the time. You and I were created with a great plan in mind, but we will know that plan and experience the exhilaration of living it only when we find the treasure!

Finding the Big-Girl treasure within requires desire, openness, curiosity, and courage. Wherever you are in your process of finding it, I pray that you will allow God to turn your heart toward becoming more and more what He intends you to be: a Big Girl!

> *Turn my heart toward your statutes*
> *and not toward my selfish gain.*
> PSALM 119:36 NIV

One

God's Heart for His Girls

He Is Crazy About You and Has Really Big Plans

W HEN I WAS A LITTLE GIRL, I hated to put on the tight little cotton socks that were part of a four-year-old girl's wardrobe in those days. My daddy knew I hated the pulling and the tugging. I often dawdled when I should have been dressing myself, so mornings were a hassle for me and my parents. I just didn't like those socks.

I remember the relief I felt one morning when I came half awake and realized that my daddy was putting my socks on for me. His help made it so much easier for me to face the day. I didn't have to do what I hated!

At the time, I was a little girl with a little girl's perspective on socks. I didn't like them, and there was nothing in me that was going to come around to seeing the necessity of struggling to put those socks on. Knowing my struggle and my little-girl immaturity, my daddy had compassion on me. He came in my room and put my socks on my sleepy little feet every morning for months before he left for work.

When I was old enough to handle the sock situation, though, he stopped helping me out. I could put on my own socks, and so I did. To continue helping me would have crippled my maturity. I needed to grow, to become stronger, more mature and more responsible. He stepped aside, to my advantage.

God has the same heart toward His girls. His plan for us is that we will grow up, not just from little girls to big girls, but from Little Girls to Big Girls who can step into all He desires us to be. Throughout the process He is always with us, gently nudging us with compassion and help until we can "get it" for ourselves.

If you really knew what God had in mind for you before you were born, you would be blown away. Read these words that are all about you, and then we'll take a look at what God had in mind for His girls.

> You made all the delicate, inner parts of my body
>> and knit me together in my mother's womb.
> Thank you for making me so wonderfully complex!
>> Your workmanship is marvelous—and how well I know it.
> You watched me as I was being formed in utter seclusion,
>> as I was woven together in the dark of the womb.
> You saw me before I was born.
>> Every day of my life was recorded in your book.
> Every moment was laid out
>> before a single day had passed.
> How precious are your thoughts about me, O God!
>> They are innumerable!
> I can't even count them;
>> they outnumber the grains of sand!
> And when I wake up in the morning,
>> you are still with me! (Psalm 139:13–18 NLT)

God loves us beyond knowing. That is sometimes hard to believe, because we can't see God in the flesh, but every word of this passage is true. Three years ago, I went with my pregnant daughter-in-law to get a 3-D baby scan. She had been through the usual sonograms, but none of them showed us the baby's face. This time, we hoped for a clearer view of her firstborn. The room was dark and the monitor was hazy as the technician rolled the scanning bar across her belly. Then we saw it: Baby Rachel's face appeared on the screen. Her eyes, her nose, her little chubby cheeks, and even her hair standing straight up! How amazed we were. Before Rachel left her mommy's womb, we knew her.

When Rachel was born, we recognized her because we had seen her before. There she was, uniquely herself with her hair standing straight up! When her daddy laid her in my arms, I recognized the face that had been knit together deep in her mama's belly. I was thrilled finally to know this amazing

> **Big-Girl Truth to Live By:**
>
> *You will never be able to count all of God's thoughts toward you! You are loved beyond all knowing.*

little baby, whom I had seen even before she had come into the light of day. That early glimpse took my breath away and only made me love her more when I first held her. Later, I thought, *If I can feel that surge of incredible joy over the birth of one of my little granddaughters, how much greater is the Father-heart of God toward His girls?*

Just imagine how heaven grew silent and His heart must have swelled with joy when—"Whaaaaaaaa!"—you had arrived on earth to become, to be, to live! Another baby girl, created by Him, was born! God is crazy about you! From the moment of your conception, He hovered over every week of your growth in the womb as you came to resemble more and more the person He designed you to be. He watched intently as you made your way into the world, screaming, writhing, and adjusting to earth's air. His complex little girl had been launched on her journey, which already was recorded in His book.

He knew your beginning.

He knew the family that would shape you.

And yes, He even knew the struggles you would have along the way.

He knew them then and He knows them now. You can say without doubt,

> How precious are your thoughts about me, O God!
>   They are innumerable!
> I can't even count them;
>   they outnumber the grains of sand!
> And when I wake up in the morning, you
>   are still with me!

He doesn't leave you during the night. He doesn't get busy and forget you are here facing challenges. He is with you!

God Knew What He Was Doing When He Created You

No matter how long your journey has been so far, He has been beside you every step of the way, hovering, listening, standing back and watching, and waiting. Perhaps He has even shed tears for you, His complex little creation, because He, like any good father, will never overpower your will. He launches you. He watches you. He loves you. He longs for a relationship with you, but He never forces it. He shows you the best way and then waits to see if you will choose it.

God created you and equipped you to make good choices, but sometimes you, like all of us, take detours and make messes that bring you pain. Sometimes life inflicts pain without your help. Circumstances and people dash hopes, divert dreams, and betray love. Even so, He always wants the best for you, always calls you to a higher place, always makes a way for you to become the woman He has in mind. His sweet promise to shape your life lovingly will never fail:

> That's why we can be so sure that every detail in our lives of love for God is worked into something good.
>
> God knew what he was doing from the very beginning. He decided from the outset to shape the lives of those who love him along the same lines as the life of his Son. The Son stands first in the line of humanity he restored. We see the original and intended shape of our lives there in him. (Romans 8:28–29 MSG)

So what does God have planned for you?

What does He call you to?

What does He want you to accomplish on your journey?

What does He want to accomplish for you?

I believe we take these questions with us through life. On certain days we may sense that we know what He wants for us; on others the answers to those questions are nothing but a big puzzle. Whether we know the answers or not, we can rest in the confidence that God is with us. The older we become, the easier it is to see how He connects the dots, to recognize how He has moved us from one event to the other, from one acquaintance to another, and from one circumstance to another. Nothing is out of His view, nothing is out of His care, and nothing is out of the range of His promise recorded in Romans 8:28–29.

When you make the choice to love God as best you can, God will take care of tucking His great plan for you into the details of your life. He wants you to become the great and gracious woman He intended. As He had plans for His Son here on earth, He has plans for you. They may be different from what you expected, but as you grow and mature—as you make the emotional, spiritual, and mental transformation from Little Girl to Big Girl—you will find yourself letting go of your preconceived notions and resting in His good plan for you. Little girls have dreams that are frequently unrealistic or simply not the best. When I was a little girl, I had the lofty dream of becoming an obstetrician, never mind that when it came to science courses, I was challenged, to say the least. But I just *knew* that I could be birthing babies all the days of my life. I still love to watch babies being born on TV, but that is about all that is left over from my little-girl days. I had some "want tos" for my life, but God had another idea. I've learned that He gives us not only the "want to" but the "how to" if our desire is really His plan. He works in you to will and to do His good pleasure (Philippians 2:13). The key to it all is to be mature enough to recognize that His good pleasure is best. Your good pleasure is second best or maybe even disastrous, but those are truths we learn along the way.

> **Big-Girl Truth to Live By:**
>
> *God always wants the best for you, always calls you to a higher place, always makes a way for you to become the woman He has in mind.*

MATURITY IS GOD'S PLAN

God never created anything to remain in an immature state. Last spring, when a bird chose the wreath on my front door as her nesting spot, I got to see this truth up close and personal. I watched the whole process of baby-bird launching with amazement. When those little birds hatched out of their shells, they were perfectly healthy and full of potential, but they weren't mature enough yet to fly. They looked like birds, they cheeped like birds, and they had all the equipment of birds, but they couldn't do what birds are created to do—fly! Only when they grew up would they know the purpose of their existence. They would be a real, live bird (or, I could say, a Big Bird!) The mother bird (having matured herself) knew this. Consequently, for a limited time, she put her life on hold and nurtured the peeping young birds until their feathers began to grow. At that point, the mature mama bird began stripping the nest of its soft materials. She withheld food from the fledglings, and then (I held my breath) she withdrew her protection. I watched, hoping and praying she knew what she was doing. These birds were hanging in a wreath above a cement porch. The cat who lives here knew it. I almost couldn't watch, but I also couldn't *not* watch.

Then, as if on the appointed day, in a big flurry of hope and determination, somehow Mama Bird made those little balls of fluff and feathers believe that choosing to fly away was more appealing than choosing to stay in the only home they had ever known. She knew if they stayed there, they would soon die. She insisted they choose maturity. It was the only way they would survive.

Birds don't have a choice about whether to grow up or not. Either they do or they die. They live and survive by instinct, knowing inherently what to choose. It's that simple.

We people, on the other hand, can decide whether to grow up or to stay immature. Because of God's nature, He has given His humans the free will to choose our responses to what happens in our lives and our feelings about Him. He gives us everything we need for life and godliness and then waits to see if we will choose it. Unlike birds, people live and survive by *wisdom,* a gift that always requires us to choose one thing over another. We can choose to be wise or we can choose to be foolish. (The consequences, however, are not ours to choose.) And unlike instinct, wisdom is *learned.* We have to learn what we must do to be wise, then make the choice to embrace what we have learned, and ultimately practice it as a way of life. This is the journey we take from immaturity to maturity.

Immaturity longs to be older, wiser, bigger, and more in control; maturity is being older, wiser, bigger, and more in control. Immaturity is dependence; maturity is independence. Immaturity is impulsive choices based on emotional reactions; maturity is thoughtful, sound choices. Maturity is full experience and delight. Hands down, maturity is the preferred state.

It is always fascinating to think that there is some wonderful plan for our lives, if only we can find it. Well, we can find it and live it. I love the scripture that says, "'For I know the plans I have for you,' declares the LORD, 'plans to prosper you and not to harm you, plans to give you hope and a future'" (Jeremiah 29:11 NIV). The finding and the living hang on my choice to cooperate with God.

I want to become the full-grown, fully mature, grace-filled woman that He envisioned before I was even born.

I want to be the full-size, grown-up version of that wonder-filled baby girl He knit together in my mother's womb.

I want to be so in tune with Him and His thoughts and ideas

for me that I can know and celebrate on a daily basis that I am fearfully and wonderfully made.

I want His dream for me to be a reality.

Do you want anything less? I doubt it. The question is, how do we find this "future and hope?"

The great thing about becoming a Big Girl is that God knows we are *becoming*. You don't discover the whole life all at once. God is such a loving Father that He doesn't condemn us for what we are not. Just as you don't condemn the three-year-old children in your life for not knowing how to tie their shoes, your Father doesn't expect you to know and do what you are not big enough to handle. That is not His way. This great God of ours works in us to make us all we can be. He does not just sit on the sidelines waiting for us to trip up while we try to be a bigger girl than we are. He just longs for us to grow and live each season of our lives to the max, and He empowers us to do it if we really want to.

And that's what being a Big Girl is all about: living life to the fullest in all ways, in all places, and in all situations.

We have embarked on a journey—a journey to become all that we can be with all that we have been given. This is not an adventure for the fainthearted, you'll see, for becoming a Big Girl means that you will have to examine your beliefs, your thoughts, your motives, your actions, and your speech. The journey might rock your world. Some people in your life might not want to relate to you as a Big Girl. They may like you better as a Little Girl. Finding you living as a Big Girl who knows who she is and what she is about may cause them to question themselves and your relationship. They may go so far as to question your heart, your motives, and your authenticity. Let me assure you, it's all right.

When you grow, things are never the same. You can't escape change. Once you have become a Big Girl, you will love it so much, there is no way you will go back to being a Little Girl, no matter who is confused and unhappy about it. Some people just can't handle change, even when it is good. That is why nature has us beat all over the place with its patient acceptance of change.

I've never seen a tree try to go back to being a seedling. The glory of the tree is being a full-grown, fully mature tree.

I've never seen a grown bird try to nestle into a nest in order to become a dependent chick once more. The glory of the bird is to be able to fly and ultimately to care for its own little ones.

I've never seen a fully-opened rose try to make itself into a tight little bud once more.

Such reversal goes against all the laws of nature and the great heart of God. He longs for all of His creation to be all it can be, and the fulfillment of this vision only comes as we reach full maturity.

What do you think? Do you want to go for the journey? Do you want to find out what being a Big Girl is all about? Then come with me. The adventure has only begun.

Two

Are You a Big Girl or a Little Girl?

The Behaviors That Define Us

Diane's brothers all live within several miles of her home. Every Thanksgiving and Christmas they arrive at her house ready to celebrate. Their wives bring a casserole, but the major responsibility for the events lies on Diane's shoulders. She has complained to her husband, whined to her girlfriends, and pouted with her brothers, but she is quick to say, "They just don't get it!"

The reality is, Diane doesn't get it. She is acting like a little girl who has no choices! Little Girls have decisions made for them; Big Girls make decisions. Diane can control what happens at her house at Thanksgiving and Christmas. She does not have to keep doing the same thing every year just because that's the way her family has always done things or because her brothers expect it. Diane can make some choices, but inside she feels she can't. After all, what would happen if her brothers became angry with her? What if they don't want to change the way things are? What if her sisters-in-law resented her? What if? What if? What if? Diane is a Little Girl who will be amazed at how delighted she will be when she makes the choices required to grow up and be a Big Girl. What a difference those choices will make!

Right down the street is Marcia, who has three kids under the age of twelve living at her house. She is a grown woman and a mom, but in her home she asks her eldest daughter, Samantha, to make a lot of the Big Girl decisions that really belong to Marcia. Twelve-year-old Samantha decides what her two brothers will eat. She prepares their lunches for school and makes sure their clothes are kept clean. She looks after them as much as a twelve-year-old can, but she really wishes her mom would be a mom to her and to the boys. Samantha also has a fifteen-year-old boyfriend who is at the house way too much, but Marcia doesn't say anything about his comings and goings. She doesn't want to interfere because Samantha is so responsible. Marcia feels it would be too intrusive to insist on a new arrangement with Sam's boyfriend. Marcia is sweet, but she doesn't think she can ask too much from the children, and she really doesn't think she has much to give. This household needs a Big Girl in charge, and that doesn't mean the twelve-year-old.

Across town lives Donna. She loves her husband, Randy, and there is no doubt that he loves her. They have been married for twenty years, and Donna doesn't want to function by herself in almost any arena. If she goes to the grocery store, Randy goes with her. If she shops for clothes, Randy holds her purse while she is in the fitting room. If she goes to the doctor, Randy sits in the waiting room. Randy accommodates Donna because she has convinced him that she can't function without him. She needs him to be by her side in almost every activity she might pursue outside the house. In fact, when they changed churches, Randy sat with Donna in the ladies' Sunday school class until she decided she could handle going on her own. Unfortunately, Randy and Donna have three teenage daughters who believe their daddy has to do everything for them, too. The two who are drivers have never put gas in a car. Randy has always done it for them. For Randy's emotional health as well as for her own, Donna needs to find the Big Girl inside her, and she needs to show her daughters how to find theirs as well.

In that church with Donna is Gina, a woman who has a lot and enjoys it all. That is why it is puzzling to see her struggle—for months—over whether she should paint her bedroom a deep burgundy or a slate blue. She admits the decision-making process is driving her crazy. "I know what I want the bedroom to look like, but I just can't make up my mind about the color." This topic has come up more than once over the course of several months. Will the bedroom be burgundy or

> **Big-Girl Truth to Live By:**
>
> *Until you take responsibility for yourself, you cannot become all God hopes you will be.*

blue? Which will it be? Gina needs the Big Girl inside her to step up to the plate and make the decision, but for the life of her, she can't find that Big Girl. I really believe she is in there; Gina just doesn't know how to let her out.

Diane, Marcia, Donna, and Gina all have something in common: They have never grown up and embraced the joy of being a Big Girl. They are clinging to vestiges of immaturity that for some reason have served them well in the past and continue to be called upon in the here and now. The problem is, these women aren't functioning at their maximum. Until the Big Girl inside each of them steps up and takes responsibility for herself and her life assignment (the people who are dependent on her guidance, help, and love, and the circumstances that need her attention and intervention) these women cannot become all God desires for them in His heart.

WHAT IS A LITTLE GIRL?

I love to read books on the different personality types. The material comes in many forms, but the bottom line for just about all of them is that if you have certain characteristics, you will consistently respond to life situations in certain ways. The key word in that statement is "consistently." A Big Girl is consistent in the way she responds. You don't have to wonder what she will do or say. You don't have to worry on pins and needles about what kind of mood she will be in. You know what you can count on where a Big Girl is concerned.

That characteristic sets the Big Girl apart from the Little Girl. Unlike the Big Girl, the Little Girl is inconsistent in her responses to life and people. Moodiness, self-absorption, and fragile emotions characterize the Little Girl. As a consequence, one really can't know what to expect from her—except the unexpected.

Marian is a grandmother whose grown children cannot rely on her to be consistent in anything but her inconsistency. One day she may be welcoming and gracious; the next, cold and unapproachable. Because they have spent their whole lives dealing with "Mother's spells," they have written her off ever having been a woman of wisdom and virtue. When they were young, she frequently threatened suicide. Sometimes she overdosed on over-the-counter medications, though she never took enough to truly harm herself, just enough to make a point. Sometimes in the garage she sat in the car with the motor running but would turn it off in the nick of time. She would return to the kitchen and then go on as if nothing had happened. The children have vivid memories of nights when she unburdened herself to them about their father's indiscretions.

Because she was and is so self-absorbed, they never have been able to count on her to be there for them; their lot is to be there for her. There is no way they would ever be like the children of Proverbs 31, who rise up and call their Big Girl mother "blessed." Marian's children just hope they will be able to manage her unpredictable, immature behavior when she becomes older and more dependent on them. In reality, they're scared. Marian has always been dependent on someone to take care of her. She has expected it, and the people around her have bowed to her expectations.

Because Marian has made life all about her, she has created some major pain and complications for her family. Holidays were always the worst. Just when things seemed to be quiet and peaceful, a holiday would come and Marian would end up at odds with someone. If it wasn't one of her sisters, you could always count on her to have a row with her husband. Growing up is nothing she desires or even contemplates. Remember, growing inevitably brings about change, and change is the last thing Marian wants. She might have to become responsible for the things she says, thinks, and tries to reason out. That would be too big a challenge for her. Instead, she wants to make those around her responsible for what she does or doesn't do. This Little Girl has run the show for a long time. The situation she has created is one of those family tragedies that everyone regrets but no one really knows how to fix. Marian has lived the Little Girl life so well for so long that she really doesn't have eyes to see that she is stuck in immature, self-absorbed ways.

Let me give you some Little Girl characteristics to consider. Who knows? You might, as I did, find yourself popping up in the list from time to time. If you do, don't despair. A woman who wants to be a Big Girl can recognize negative characteristics in herself as well as positive ones. That lets you know you are on target with growing. You can't deal with what you don't acknowledge, right? So if you see yourself in this list, just make a note, and we will deal with your observations in the chapters to come.

A Little Girl . . .

• *Tends to be self-absorbed.* She is generally unaware of others' feelings and inflexible when it comes to accommodating others' needs. She wants to be the center of attention, whether overtly or by default. (For example, she will be the life of the party or the party pooper; either way, she gets the attention!) She takes herself way too seriously and would never dream of laughing at herself. She is convinced that others laugh at her anyway. She believes that she should be good at everything and will refuse to admit that others are better than she is at certain things. She is high-maintenance at home and in the workplace. This means the people around her serve her hand and foot if she can get them to do it, and she usually can, because she uses guilt very well. In the workplace, she doesn't keep a job for long, though she blames others for her restlessness or dissatisfaction.

• *Lacks discretion, insight, and wisdom.* She behaves inappropriately at important times and rarely thinks about consequences. She is more impulsive than thoughtful. She can be a little stingy or inappropriately lavish when giving gifts. She might flaunt her wealth or poor-mouth her poverty. She is impressed by wealthy people and can be very contemptuous of those who have less. She can't manage her financial circumstances, whatever they might be.

• *Makes others responsible for her happiness.* She is dependent upon others for her sense of value and is highly influenced by what others say. She has no realization that she—and not her friends, husband, or children—is responsible for her own happiness. She is always seeking someone's approval and becomes angry if she doesn't get it. Quite often, like Donna, she needs to be attached to someone to feel whole.

• *Avoids getting close to God.* She is angry with Him most of the time and blames Him for her troubles during pity parties, but she expects God to rescue her. She doesn't know what she believes about God, but she knows a preacher who does, and she depends on him to tell her what's what about spiritual matters. She doubts that being a woman is good. She recognizes that God has plans for others but thinks He overlooked her when handing out His favor. If she were a man, she reasons, things would be different. God seems to like men better and would never consider giving her what He gives men.

• *Has a hard time being a wife.* She relates to her spouse as if he were her daddy, a child, or an adversary. None of these approaches works, but a Little Girl has a hard time seeing her marriage any other way.

• *Has a hard time being a mother.* She either holds on to her children for too long, causing them to be needy, or she is indifferent to their needs, believing her own to be more significant. She lets her children run wild or restricts them far too much. She goes to extremes of being overly responsible or, like Marcia, dangerously irresponsible—in parenting and in other areas of her life.

• *Has a hard time being a good friend.* She can smother her friends or cut them off for minor infractions of her rules of friendship. She "uses up" one or two friends at a time, exhausting them with her expectations. She frequently becomes a taker in relationships.

•   *Takes a cynical approach to life and the future.* She believes her life to be of little value and often sees her future as quite bleak. She longs for the good old days and compares where she used to be with where she is. She refuses to admit the good old days were just "old days." She sighs as each new day begins. Life is too hard and too demanding of her. She sees her old age as a threat and does not believe she has anything of value to pass on to future generations. (Or, if she does, she believes they do not want what she has.) She does not like to think about the future other than to worry about what might be wrong with her.

Obviously, the typical Little-Girl woman doesn't exhibit all of these characteristics at once, but those that she does display are usually pretty typical of her. Those are her sticking points. The Little-Girl thoughts, reasoning, and self-talk that she clings to are the *roadblocks* to her growth, just as a Big Girl's thoughts, reasoning, and self-talk are *stepping stones* to her growth.

What Is a Big Girl?

Unlike the Little Girl, a Big Girl knows who she is. She loves the woman God created her to be, and she's willing to keep growing up. If she is twenty, she doesn't settle for living as a teenager. If she is forty, she embraces that transitional decade without holding on to her thirties in terror of the future. If she is fifty, she basks in the mellowing maturity that is at her command. If she is seventy, she begins to let go with the grace of a life well lived. A Big Girl wears her life well. No matter what circumstances comprise her life, it looks good on her.

Sherry is one of those Big Girls. She is a single mother in her forties who is responsible for her own two children as well as her sister's three children. She works as a cashier in a restaurant. There is nothing glamorous about the circumstances of her life, yet because she is living life as a Big Girl she radiates an inner beauty that is attractive to all who meet her. She is known for her steady, joyful encouragement of others. The patrons in the restaurant where she works can count on being blessed and encouraged just because they will see Sherry when they check out. Many of the regulars carry on small talk with her every time they come in. She knows their children and grandchildren by name and shares their joys and sorrows. Few of them know Sherry's story, and no one would know by her demeanor the huge life assignment she has. Being handed a weighty responsibility that she didn't ask for has given her the opportunity to find out what she is made of and to live with full confidence in God as only a Big Girl can. Sherry allows the Big Girl inside of her to live every day. It is her choice. It is her joy.

Below is a collection of traits that personify the Big Girl. Clearly, she stands opposite the Little Girl in almost every regard. There are more traits, I'm sure, but these are some to consider. See if you can see an emerging profile in this list.

A Big Girl . . .

• *Cares more about others than herself.* She is sensitive to others as well as to their needs. She is flexible, caring, and kind. She is generous toward those who have less than she, and she doesn't patronize those who have more. She treats others well and expects to be treated well herself. She is an asset in the workplace. She doesn't whine!

• *Possesses remarkable discretion, insight, and wisdom.* She is sensible and reasonable. Her advice is generally sound and reliable. She knows when to speak and when to stay silent. She doesn't mind being the center of attention if necessary but doesn't force herself into the spotlight when it belongs on someone else. She knows how to handle herself in social situations that could be uncomfortable. She doesn't take herself too seriously; she can laugh at herself and laugh with others. She recognizes that everything she does has a consequence. She thoughtfully considers the consequences before she makes a move. She is responsible and holds herself accountable, but she recognizes the things for which she is responsible and the things for which she is not. If she falters, she does what she can to rectify the situation and then she moves on. She doesn't spend hours on end, as Diane does, in the "if only" and "what if" patch.

• *Understands that she is responsible for her own happiness.* She is comfortable in her own skin, at her own age, in her own place in history. She doesn't need to seek approval from others, and she doesn't need to have a significant other to feel significant. She is not afraid to be herself with her husband or with any of her family members. She lives authentically because she believes she has nothing to lose and nothing to prove. She knows what she does well and what she doesn't do so well and admits both easily. She is keen to improve what she does poorly if she needs to. What she doesn't need to do well, she leaves alone.

• *Invites God to be part of all that she does.* She also accepts God's invitation to be part of all that *He* does. She loves and respects God and isn't afraid of Him. She is comfortable with God whether her days are good or bad. She doesn't dogmatically cling to her beliefs. Instead, she knows what she believes but is open to learning more and even to being corrected. She loves being a woman and recognizes her place in the grand plan of her loving Lord.

• *Embraces her role as a wife.* She treats her husband with respect. But she doesn't put him on a pedestal off of which he will surely fall. She understands and honors the roles she and her husband play in their marriage. She knows those roles are part of God's plan, and she knows they work best even on days of wishing He had another plan. (After all, Big Girls are human, too.)

• *Understands what it means to be a good mother.* When she becomes a mother she accepts that she is the mother and the child is the child. She keeps her children in check while they are under her roof and are her responsibility. She never tries to make her child responsible for being anything but a child. For example, she never puts her personal burdens on her children. She does not allow them to feel as if they need to be her confidant or her protector. She lets them be children. When they become adults, she lets her children go. She knows that this is good and natural, and she won't let herself pine away for their childhood. She can miss them, but she doesn't constantly remind them that she wishes they were still at home. Big Girls let their children go!

• *Delights in being a good friend.* She knows how to have a friendship without the bondage of hyper-expectation. She contributes to her friends' lives instead of draining them. She gives space to her friends but draws close to them when needed. She knows and appreciates the value of "the group." She has many friends because she has been a friend to many.

• *Sees her life as valuable but fleeting.* She looks to the future knowing she will leave a legacy whether good or bad. She avoids looking back and longing for "the good old days." She can appreciate the past but she looks at each new day as "the day which the LORD has made" and she rejoices and is glad in it (see Psalm 118:24). She sees her old age as precious, and heaven as her ultimate destination.

Does this look like the person you want to become? If so, we'll spend the rest of the book talking about how you can "grow there" from where you are today. As we do, keep in mind that true Big Girls aren't perfect. Neither you nor I will have all of these qualities operating at the same time. Being a Big Girl means that you know you are really a Big Girl in process. You are well aware that you have not arrived. You are certain that there is always more growth and more change, but you view being a Big Girl as the opportunity *now* to live the life God dreamed for you! Just knowing that this kind of life is available to the Big Girl makes the required stretching and growing so much more appealing.

Why Don't We Keep Growing Automatically?

With such possibilities lying ahead, why do so many of us stop short of the fullness God intends for each of us? I believe we get comfortable in our immaturity *because it seems to work,* and too many of us cling to the trite statement, "If it isn't broken, don't fix it." What we fail to realize is that sometimes we don't know what is broken. We understand discomfort, failure, and difficult relationships, but it doesn't dawn on us that our own immaturity could be to blame or that life can be better than it is now.

Let's go back for a moment to another lesson from the birds. (I watch birds out my office window all day while I work; thus, so many bird stories!) When the weather gets rough and strong winds begin to blow, birds seek refuge and batten down the hatches. They don't protect themselves based on how they feel, or on whether they want to or not, or on what all the other birds are doing. Remember, they're driven by instinct. Their "get out of danger" instinct tells them what to do, and they do it. During a storm you won't see one single bird. But when the storm passes by, it doesn't take long for them to come out again—unscathed, undaunted, and grateful to be out foraging for food once more.

We humans, on the other hand, often foolishly decide to party in the middle of storms. We refuse to take shelter because we don't feel like it, or because we think we are smarter than those who say, "There is a

> **Big-Girl Truth to Live By:**
>
> *Making the choice to pursue maturity can fix a lot of what is broken in your life, even when you don't recognize your brokenness.*

storm coming." This lack of wisdom is the mark of immaturity. Remember, what the birds know to do by instinct, we know to do by wisdom. But wisdom by its very nature resides only in the hearts of the mature; that is, those who are in the process of finding their full potential.

God wants His women to be mature. Let's face it: We are an easier bunch to deal with when we choose to leave behind our Little-Girl ways. Making that choice to pursue maturity can fix a lot of what is broken in our lives, even when we don't recognize our brokenness.

CHOOSING MATURITY BRINGS HEALING AND STABILITY

Hannah Whitall Smith, author of *The Christian's Secret of a Happy Life*, was a woman of profound influence in her time as well as today. "From the time of her conversion in 1858 until her death more than fifty years later in 1911, [she] served as a spiritual guide

for thousands of Christians," write Melvin and Hallie Dieter in
God Is Enough. Hannah didn't become that woman of influence
naturally or overnight. She was born into a prosperous family who
practiced a barren religion that left her with no answers. When
she and her husband, Robert Pearsall Smith, came to have a living
relationship with the Lord Jesus Christ, she found a new source of
hope. But even then, everything was not wonderful. She struggled
with her longing for some physical evidence that she truly knew
Jesus. Robert struggled with emotional highs and lows that left
both of them wondering what was going on. Life wasn't what
Hannah thought it would be.

But at that point, "She finally came to the unshakable convic-
tion that faith in Jesus Christ as we know Him in the sure and true
words of the Bible is the only steady foundation for the Christian
life."[1] In other words, Hannah came to believe, even in her pursuit
of certainty, that *faith* was the stabilizing message of Scripture.
She chose to take God at His Word. She chose to recognize that
He was always with her. She chose to believe that He is a loving
Father. These choices enabled her to grasp the life for which God
had created her.

Hannah Whitall Smith was a Big Girl who "got it," and as a
result, enabled others to "get it" as well. Despite the challenges of
her circumstances, she chose to live in what she called "the optimism of grace" and in so doing found a place where Big Girls can
feel at home. We can get a glimpse of Hannah's Big Girl thinking
from some of her writing (which, by the way, would not have been
particularly acceptable in her day):

> The old mystics used to teach what they called "detachment,"
> meaning the cutting loose of the soul from all that could hold
> it back from God. The need for detachment is the secret of

much of our instability. We cannot follow the Lord fully so long as we are tied fast to anything else, any more than a boat can sail out into the boundless ocean so long as it is tied fast to the shore.[2]

Hannah could have spent years lamenting the fact that although she came from a prosperous home where she was deeply loved, she had the odd fortune to marry a man who was wildly unpredictable. Instead, she chose the path of maturity. She decided to be a Big Girl, and consequently she was able to live the adventure God had planned for her with contentment and peace.

The stability of a Big Girl's life doesn't come just because you would like to have it. You must choose to pursue it. The pursuit might be difficult, and your choices—even though good—will have consequences, but often the hard choices are the ones that ultimately make life easier. Big Girls know that. Big Girls who love God and who know they are loved recognize that He will cause every hard choice to work together for good. Remember, He is vitally interested in every step of your way.

Hannah Whithall Smith found what every Big Girl ultimately discovers: Your happiness and fulfillment is linked to the way that you think. Emotions are feelings that originate with what you think. So if you get in a tough spot and think you are going to lose your cool, you will lose your cool. If you think, "I'm going to blow my stack," your emotions will erupt and you will blow your stack. If you say to yourself, "I can't handle this," then you probably won't be able to handle it. Your emotions will kick in and you will "feel" exactly what you have thought. If you declare to a friend or foe, "You make me so mad," then your mad emotions will take over, and you will probably say and do things you don't mean because you think another person has the power to make you mad. You may not like what other people do, but they cannot make you "feel" a certain way unless you cognitively decide to feel that way.

After choosing the path of maturity, Big Girls know and understand that the first change they must master is to bring their thoughts, emotions, and speech under control. That's what we'll tackle next.

Three

How a Big Girl Speaks,
How a Big Girl Thinks

Putting Away Little-Girl Ways

I REMEMBER A NIGHT in my late twenties when a discussion about a toothbrush brought about a life-altering change in my maturity.

Charlie, my husband, had spent the better part of the day cleaning the shower in our bathroom. When it was time to go to bed, I could not find my toothbrush, and so I asked him if he knew where it was. He, of course, denied any knowledge of my toothbrush. Well *he* may not have known anything about it, but *I* knew it had been there in the morning, and I knew that between then and bedtime, he had used a brush to clean the shower. Instead of being grateful that the shower had been meticulously cleaned, and instead of applying the wisdom of abandoning the quarrel before it begins (see Proverbs 17:14), I chose to make my point. Relentlessly.

I became a virtual Perry Mason. "Well, if you didn't take my toothbrush, then who did? You used a brush. Where did you get it? If you didn't use my toothbrush, then whose brush did you use?" By the time my inquisition reached fever pitch, Charlie got out of bed, pulled his pants on, threw on a shirt, and walked out the front door without a word. That made me mad, but I thought, *Good, he's gone.*

Then I heard the tearful voice of a little boy crying in the next room. I had no idea that one of our sons was awake and had heard the whole exchange. Not only had he listened to his Little-Girl mother natter on about her toothbrush, he heard his daddy leave abruptly in what was for this young child the middle of the night. His little mind had to be confused and hurting. He was trying to figure out what on earth was going on in his family. I went to his room to try to comfort him. He was crying in his pillow, sobbing, "My daddy is gone and he's not coming back." I assured him that his daddy would be back and that everything was fine; we had just been talking about a toothbrush. (A ridiculous explanation, but the best I had to offer.) He quieted down, and I went back to our room to seethe until Charlie returned.

I soon heard his key in the lock and his footsteps on the stairs. He came into our room, tossed six new toothbrushes on the bed and calmly said, "Brush your teeth and let's go to bed." Well, I brushed my teeth and I went to bed, but I couldn't sleep for thinking about the little boy, my precious son, who had been profoundly affected by his mother's Little-Girl stand. Right or wrong, I had made a choice that had wounded the youngest, most vulnerable member of our family.

That incident marked the beginning of significant growth for me. Being faced with the stark reality about yourself is often the first step toward growing up and wanting to leave behind your childish ways. In fact, I would say, it is the best and only way to learn. When you see yourself for who you are and for what you are doing, the choice to change becomes evident. I had to face the reality that I would have to put away my childish speaking, or people I loved were going to be profoundly, permanently affected.

Now, it took me a while to understand that the choice to *change* was mine, but the actual *changing* was something that God would have to do in me. He allows life circumstances to do the convincing, and then He lovingly, graciously comes along and does for us and in us what we cannot do for ourselves. I could want to change; I could decide to change; I could modify my behavior, but God had to accomplish the permanent change that I could depend on. I could put away the thing I didn't like to do; but God is the one who could lock the cupboard door.

I have since come to love 1 Corinthians 13:11, which says, "When I was a child, I spoke and thought and reasoned as a child does. But when I grew up, I put away childish things" (NLT). I realize this verse appears in the context of spiritual gifts, but truth is truth no matter the context. If doing away with childish things is relevant to spiritual gifts, surely it is relevant to life as well.

I Used to Speak Like a Child

The tongue is one of the first markers of maturity. If you want to give yourself a personal maturity checkup, you can begin by listening to yourself. How do you speak? What is the tone of what you say? Do you sound the way you want to sound, or do you sound like a whiny little girl? Your words are a dead giveaway, especially if you are tired, hungry, or just plain ticked. Little-Girl speech can be defined as saying what you want to say, when you want to say it, to whomever you want to say it. It takes no one else into consideration. It is speech that is useful to achieve certain kinds of short-term goals, but in the long term, it is always costly. The Little Girl in you will want to be heard and may blurt out things she really doesn't mean. With practice, you might even recognize what's happening and hear yourself say, "Where did that come from?" Well, my dear, it came from you, your will, and your emotions.

> **Big-Girl Truth to Live By:**
>
> *You can always add to a conversation at the appropriate time, but you never can erase words once spoken.*

The Big Girl knows that her speech matters. She knows that she has the power of life and death in her tongue (see Proverbs 18:21), so she uses it very carefully, knowing it is like a loaded weapon. She remembers in all situations, "Reckless words pierce like a sword" (Proverbs 12:18 NIV). There is nothing worse than having to go back and eat your words, wishing you hadn't said something. You can always add to a conversation at the appropriate time, but you never can erase words once spoken. That is something a Big Girl knows and lives by. She doesn't always have to be heard. Her words are circumspect, because she knows that one of the first places a girl reveals her authentic self—Big or Little—is in her speech.

As I discovered in my own life, a Big Girl also knows that God is the change agent who is there to lovingly alter her speech patterns. She has to recognize and admit the need for change. She has to want to change and then ask God to do the changing in her. That is how it can be done. That is how it works. Change is not a big self-effort campaign. God is faithful to fulfill the desires of an obedient heart. When you revert to Little-Girl ways, admit it, ask forgiveness, and then get on with it. Don't wallow in the "Oh, I'm such a bad girl" mud. That is a royal waste of time. Big Girls are Little Girls who own up to their stuff and let God change them.

He can change you just like He has changed millions of your sisters. You just have to want to change and invite Him into the process.

I Used to Think Like a Child

Our speech is governed at least in part by the way we think. Thinking is the engine that pulls along every emotion you have. I am passionate about women learning to think like Big Girls. So many of us have never abandoned childish ways of thinking, and therefore we find ourselves overwhelmed with childish emotions and childish speech. The Big Girl knows that her capacity to think is her greatest asset. Mature thinking produces mature living, and of course childish thinking produces childish living. You have only to stop and observe about how the children you know think, and you will see the problem.

- Children don't think things through to their natural conclusion. They see only what is immediate.

- Children don't think about how their actions will affect others.

- Children are unable to see more than one side to any situation.

- Children take things personally. "She hurt my feelings." "That's my doll." "He hit me."

- Children really like it best when "it's all about me."

- Children are better manipulators than negotiators. They learn early how to manipulate and whom to manipulate.

- Children like fairy tales where good guys always win, bad guys always lose, and everyone lives happily ever after.

- Children tire easily and allow fatigue to affect their general attitude and demeanor.

- Children do not know what is best for them, although they may protest loudly when they fail to get what they want.

These are just some of the ways that children think. Little Girls, even though they're grown women, still cling to these childish ways. But when a Big Girl asks God to work in her and learns to replace the old ways with mature thinking, she can begin to put away her childish thoughts and will notice an incredible difference in her life. Here are some ways to challenge your thinking as a Big Girl in process. (It is always good to have a standard by which to check yourself.)

- Big Girls think things through to their natural conclusion. They see not only the present but the future as well.

- Big Girls think about how their actions will affect others.

- Big Girls can see more than one side to any situation.

- Big Girls don't take things personally. They understand someone can only hurt you emotionally if you let them.

- Big Girls understand that life is never "all about me."

- Big Girls are good, fair, and reasonable negotiators.

- Big Girls may like fairy tales, but they like true stories, too, and are well aware of the difference.

- Big Girls may tire, but they don't allow their fatigue to control their general attitude and demeanor.

- Big Girls know what is best for them and are disciplined enough to go after it.

I love Philippians 4. I have labeled it the Big Girl chapter in my Bible. It so clearly spells out the thoughts and attitudes of a Big Girl. There is nothing like the Word of God for making it clear. Look at these verses and see if you can see a Big Girl thread running though them.

BIG GIRLS STAND FIRM IN THE LORD

Therefore, my beloved brethren [I like to think he included "sistern," too!] whom I long to see, my joy and crown, in this way stand firm in the Lord, my beloved. (Philippians 4:1)

Big Girls plant their spiritual feet firmly in the Lord. They don't waffle back and forth between "He loves me, He loves me not." They determine to be joined to the Lord through the bridge provided by the Lord Jesus Christ. Every Big Girl who has made that decision comes to the point where she realizes that she cannot do things on her own. Like everyone else in the world, she cannot keep God's law perfectly.

When Jesus Christ, God in human form, willingly hung on the cross to pay for every sin you and I ever committed or ever will commit, He made a bridge for us to get back to God. We are all sinners, separated from God (see Romans 3:23). So He did for us what we can never do for ourselves. We can never be religious enough or go to church enough or pray enough or give enough to free ourselves from being unable to perfectly keep God's law and therefore reach God. It is impossible. The Bible says, "For whoever keeps the whole law and yet stumbles in one point, he has become guilty of all" (James 2:10).

Think about something as simple as a speed limit. If the law says go twenty-five miles an hour and you go twenty-six miles an hour, even if you *meant* to go twenty-five miles an hour, you are guilty of breaking the law. No flexibility. That is the way the law operates. Big Girls know they can't keep God's law perfectly, so they recognize their need for a Savior and accept the free gift of eternal life that comes through Jesus Christ. Once it is done, it is done. She stands firm no matter what wind blows. In other words, she chooses to position herself in such a way that she will not get knocked over by failure or discouragement or anything else that might rob her of the life she has found in Jesus. She plants her feet in the truth of John 6:37: "All that the Father gives Me will come to Me, and the one who comes to Me I will certainly not cast out." Once you have come to the Father, your life in Him is a done deal. You can stand firm!

BIG GIRLS OVERLOOK TRANSGRESSIONS

I urge Euodia and I urge Syntyche to live in harmony in the Lord. (Philippians 4:2)

I love this one. It would seem Euodia and Syntyche had trouble with this harmony thing. These two girls probably squabbled, and now their little disagreement has been recorded in holy writ for all time. (How would you like that?) Think about it. When we all get to heaven and are introduced to E or S, wouldn't you like to ask each one what their take on the little tiff was? I know we won't be thinking about those things in heaven, but I do wonder if we had two Little Girls here trying to be the center of attention. Whatever happened, they managed to get themselves written up. The truth is, Big Girls overlook transgressions. They don't spend a lot of time on the little stuff. They cut each other a lot of slack and recognize that no two women are going to see things the same way. They don't enable bad behavior by allowing it to continue on an ongoing basis, but when those little bumps and bruises occur that are part of living, Big Girls take the high road. They overlook whatever has been done and cover it. "He who conceals a transgression seeks love, but he who repeats a matter separates intimate friends" (Proverbs 17:9).

Women who work together have incredible opportunities to cover or overlook transgressions. They spend more time together in the workplace than most of them spend with their own families. So the chances of slights and affronts are quite high. Sarah was the office manager in a doctor's office. She had an amazing ability to let things roll off her back, and, consequently, she set the tone for others in her workplace as well. Her office was known for being a great place to work. She worked with several women staff members as well as three doctors and all of the patients. Hardly a day went by that someone didn't come to her with an annoyance concerning someone else in the practice or one of the patients. Sarah always listened warmly to whatever was being said. If one person was upset at another for petty reasons, she often would disarm the situation by saying, "I hear what you are saying and I am so sorry you have been hurt or offended by so-and-so's remarks or behavior, but you know what? If you or I had to walk in her shoes for twenty-four hours, there is no telling what we would have said or done. Do you think you could cut her some slack today? If it becomes a habit, I'll go with you to talk with her, but other than that, let's give her some grace and let it go this time." Sarah's staff loved her and often came back to thank her for letting them vent and for not making a big deal out of the encounter.

BIG GIRLS REJOICE IN THE LORD

Rejoice in the Lord always; again I will say, rejoice! (Philippians 4:4.)

Attitude is everything, and Big Girls know that whatever is going on, the way they respond is crucial. Paul is not being redundant when he says, "Rejoice, and again I say *rejoice.*" He effectively creates a picture for us. Imagine the sight of a little lamb coming out of the barn and jumping up once, then jumping up again. He leaps across the fields and hills, jumping as if for the sheer fun of it. So Big Girls are to rejoice and keep on rejoicing, *not* because things are wonderful, but because of the joy that comes from knowing the Lord is in the middle of things that are going on.

I have a sister-in-law who raises fainting goats. What a contrast they are to the little leaping lambs! These goats are slightly nasty and not very pretty. They meander about, foraging for food until they are startled by life in the goat yard and then they just up and faint! They can't stand to be startled, so they don't take time to rejoice. They just faint to get away from reality. They are programmed to avoid dealing with it! They don't rejoice, nor do they complain. They just pass out and leave the situation. I think we would call this La-la Land. Humanly speaking, they are like the Little Girls who don't face the truth. They don't recognize that God is in control and in the situation that startled them. They just faint and go to La-la Land until the distress passes by. Of course, when they come to, the circumstances are still there. What good did their little escape afford? The answer is that there was none. It is just what they have learned to do.

Big Girls know that no matter how much they might want to be like Scarlet O'Hara and deal with life's realities *tomorrow,* that is no way to live. No matter your circumstances, rejoice and rejoice again, because God is the author and finisher of life. He is in the middle of everything you face, no matter what. That's what Big Girls know and hold on to.

BIG GIRLS ARE REASONABLE

Let your gentle spirit be known to all men. The Lord is near.
(Philippians 4:5)

Having a forbearing, or gentle, spirit isn't always easy. If you think of it this way, however, then maybe it will compute: "Let your sweet reasonableness be known to all men." Big Girls are reasonable. They aren't pushovers, but they can be reasoned with.

I was in a retail situation trying to make a return when I had to make a choice to let my sweet reasonableness be known to all men. I had bought the watch on a whim. It was right before Christmas as I walked through the watch department at a local store. In the bustle of Christmas, somehow the watch box was lost. That concerned me for a moment, but I knew I had my receipt. Knowing that a receipt is a ticket to ride when it comes to returns, I felt confident when I approached the counter to return my watch.

The young man who was standing

> **Big-Girl Truth to Live By:**
>
> *Your capacity to think is your greatest asset. Mature thinking produces mature living.*

behind the counter looked troubled when I explained what I wanted to do. He said, "Oh, I'm sorry but you can't bring the watch back without a box." I said, "Really? I never knew that." I asked if I could speak to his manager, knowing that a box was really a small matter. He rolled his eyes and went to get his manager.

Well, I soon knew why he rolled his eyes. I heard his manager coming before she got there. She was doing some heavy breathing as she rounded the corner. I fully expected to look up and see Darth Vader approaching. Before I could get my request out of my mouth, she firmly told me, "You cannot bring back that watch without a box." (She had a funny little sizzle that made her sound as if she was saying boxsssssssss.) I told her that I didn't have a box, but I strongly desired to return the watch. She reiterated her statement without wavering. Reasonableness was not a part of her conversation. So I said, "Where can I get a box?"

She said, "*You* will have to order one." I replied, "Well could you get me the number to call to order?" At that point, she huffed away to the bowels of the jewelry department to find the number for me to call, or (as I really believed) to occupy herself until I gave up and went away.

The young man came closer and said, "Oh, you won't believe how difficult she is. We are going to have a meeting with the store manager in about an hour about her attitude." Seeing an opportunity to get my problem taken care of, I pulled out my business card and said, "Why don't we start that meeting early? Why don't you take this to the store manager and see if he would like that." The young man was thrilled. He shivered all over himself. I didn't know he was going to do this, but on his way to summon the store manager, he walked by Darth and said, "She wants to see the manager." Well, her response was immediate and deliberate. "Give her the money back." That was all I wanted. I was reasonable and I really thought I was sweet. When the watch was returned and I was given the money back, I turned around and bought another watch that was more expensive. During the transaction the young man said, "This is the best day I've ever had. I've loved waiting on you." I had to smile. Obviously sweet reasonableness meant more to him than to Darth, but I could walk away from that situation knowing I had been a Big Girl. I hadn't lost my cool. I had been reasonable, and the mission had been accomplished. That's what it was all about.

Reasoning with a Big Girl is always a rational process. Reasoning with a Little Girl, as I had to do with the manager, is fraught with irrational thinking. Just about the time you think you have won the case, something new will pop up. I encountered this kind of thinking when I was attempting to move from one house to another many years ago. Trying to be reasonable about the moving arrangements was a nightmare, and I certainly did not have the Big Girl skills I have now. No matter what I suggested to the woman I was dealing with, she always countered. Even once we decided on something, inevitably there would be some kind of glitch. If we agreed that I could move in at 8:00 a.m. on Saturday, I'd get a call at 10:00 P.M. Friday night informing me she couldn't be out. When I tried to find a compromise by suggesting I move my stuff in around her, she claimed I was invading her space. The event was maddening, confusing, and downright frustrating. Now I know why. We weren't experiencing a clash of personalities, as I might have described it then. The reasoning of a Little Girl was the real problem. And since I dealt with it by getting angry and frustrated, I can probably say that the reasoning of two Little Girls who knew only one way to reason was at fault. I should have been more forthcoming and clear about what I expected rather than allowing her indecisiveness to determine how things would go. Being irritated didn't change a thing. Given the same circumstances today, things would be different. I would be far more decisive and the arrangements would have been agreed upon with an airtight agreement. I would not have allowed my emotions to enter into it. Wasting precious emotional energy on being irritated does nothing. I now know this and when I feel the irritation growing, I try to say to myself, "Hold on! What are you thinking?" Then I make a choice about how to respond. Thank God we live and learn, learn and grow. What a gift!

God knows most of us need to grow up and become the rational women He designed us to be. It would make His job easier. I think of the "reasoning" that we sometimes try to do with God. A Little Girl may reason that she can stomp her foot and sway God's opinion. She can be bullheaded and selfish while demanding that God does what she wants Him to do. A Big Girl makes the choice not to reason against God. She understands that she can't argue with God. He is the One in control; she is not. A Big Girl knows she doesn't have that leg to stand on. She can talk with God, and she can plead her case in front of God, but arguing is quite out of the question. She cannot take Him on as an adversary and think that somehow she can change His mind just because she isn't pleased with Him. He has the big picture in view and will do only what is best for her. Her feelings about His dealings with her are not the issue, whether she believes that or not.

Big Girls Embrace the Peace of God

Be anxious for nothing, but in everything by prayer and supplication with thanksgiving let your requests be made known to God. And the peace of God, which surpasses all comprehension, will guard your hearts and your minds in Christ Jesus. (Philippians 4:6–7)

It is hard not to be anxious, and yet Big Girls do hard things. Anxiety is a physical reaction that manifests in a dry mouth, trembling, and a little bit of panic. Anxiety does you no good. It only creates a feeling of being out of control and having absolutely no power. Knowing that about us, God invites us to tell Him all about it. Tell the One who can do something about whatever it is that has you in such a state.

He says, "Tell Me about it, tell Me what you want Me to do about it, and thank Me for hearing your requests." When you do what He asks, then He promises that things are going to get really good, beyond your understanding. You will have a peace that doesn't make sense. You will feel as if you have been caught in a roaring wind and suddenly, inexplicably, everything gets quiet. Peace will come without explanation. You won't know where it came from, and you won't know why it came. You just know it is there and will stand guard over your emotions, which include not only your thoughts but your perceptions. Peace will come and put everything under control. First, though, you must make a move of sheer obedience and say, "I am going to give all of this anxiety to God."

Today, as I am writing this chapter of the Big-Girl book, I heard some anxiety-producing news that is distressing, totally out of my control, and to the human eye looks absolutely insurmountable. I began to feel anxiety creep into my heart, and then I began to feel overwhelmed and impotent to do anything about the problem. I had a sense of panic and agitation for a few minutes, and then I began to talk to God about it. It wasn't long before the Holy Spirit, the sweet Comforter who lives in me, whispered words of peace to me. I heard, "Be still and know that I am God" (Psalm 46:10). These last few hours, every time the troubling, anxiety-producing thought occurs, peace floods in on the wings of God's comfort. "Be still and know that I am God." I have lived long enough to know that is God's final word to me. He isn't going to explain or show me how this problem will be resolved. He simply says, "Be still." So I am still, and my heart is not anxious.

BIG GIRLS DWELL ON WHAT IS TRUE

Finally, brethren, [or I should say, sistern!] whatever is true, whatever is honorable, whatever is right, whatever is pure, whatever is lovely, whatever is of good repute, if there is any excellence and if anything worthy of praise, dwell on these things. (Philippians 4:8)

Big Girls control what their minds dwell on. If you can't control anything else in your life, you can control what you think about. But when you have been buffeted by a situation that throws you, it is so easy to abdicate your control and go to your "favorite bad feeling" as my friend Lynda Elliott, a super life coach, first called it. It's the feeling that you went to as a child because you learned that it worked to help you feel better or get what you wanted. Once you are an adult, you will find that it is the first place your mind rushes when there is something troubling on your mental radar screen.

Some of us cry, some pout, some sleep, some eat chocolate, some go shopping, some withdraw, and some slam doors, some clean house, some sit and stare. You could probably fill in your own favorite bad feeling if it isn't listed here, because we all have one. Big Girls know they have a choice. Although they have a favorite bad feeling and they can readily access it, they choose not to go there. Peace is not the result of going to your favorite bad feeling; peace is the result of choosing to focus your mind on what is true and honorable and right. When you choose to do that, it is amazing how much peace will overtake your mind and heart.

Big Girls know that they have power over their minds and emotions. They have learned that it is erroneous to say, "My husband or my sister or my father makes me feel a certain way."

Why? Because how you feel about something is under your control. What you think about will determine how you feel. If you don't like how you feel, change your thinking. Circumstances rarely change, but *how you feel* about the circumstances can change dramatically as you alter the way that you think. Your thoughts are not under the control of another person. You can hear what other people say, but you don't have to take their words into your mind and dwell on them. How you feel is up to you, not to anyone else in your life.

Big Girl thinking leads to healthy emotions. As with putting away Little-Girl speech, the desire to change your thinking is a choice. At some point, all Big Girls have to deal with their thinking.

MAKING ROOM FOR GOD'S TRANSFORMING WORK

Putting away childish things is the choice we make not to comfort ourselves with the old stuff that keeps us little. We all have old stuff, but as we mature, the old stuff takes on less appeal. If you want to be all you can be by living the life you were meant to live, and fulfilling your reason for living, then the Big Girl inside who can speak, think, and reason with grace has to emerge. She can, and she will, as you make the all-important, ongoing choice to declutter your life of Little Girl habits and leave behind childish things.

In a devotion called "Giving Up and Growing Up," Hannah Whitall Smith writes:

Meekness and quietness of spirit become in time the charac-teristics of the daily life. A submissive acceptance of the will of God as it comes in the hourly events of each day is mani-fested. Pliability in the hands of God to do or to suffer all the good pleasure of His will; sweetness under provocation; calmness in the midst of turmoil and bustle; a listening to the wishes of others, an insensibility to slights and affronts; absence of worry or anxiety; deliverance from care and fear—all these and many other similar graces are invariably found to be the natural outward development of that inward life which is hid with Christ in God.[1]

It is evident that the Big Girl will only emerge in any of us as we give our Little Girl ways to God to eliminate. We see them, we don't like them, we choose against them, but He is the One who takes them out of us and replaces them with the grace and beauty of the Big Girl. That is His work, and it is lovely!

Four

Confidence for Big-Girl Singles

Embracing the Single Life in Any Season

WHEN I WAS A PRETEEN, my idol was a woman who was single. Her name was Edna. I loved everything about her. She was stylish, kind, and brave enough to leave a good-paying clerical job in order to go to seminary. She wanted to minister in the inner city and became a social worker among the disadvantaged in Washington, D.C. She was fascinating. Edna chose what she wanted to do and she did it! Through her, I saw that singleness provided a woman with options. Although I wanted to be married and have children, I certainly did not see the single life as negative, just different.

Since those days, some of my closest friends have been singles. Most of them have been healthy, happy, and content with the single life. I call them my Big-Girl single friends. They love life and live it to the max, find ways to be connected with others, and spend very little time thinking about whether they have a significant other or not. That just isn't the focus of their lives. For some single women, however, the fact that they do not have a husband is a huge issue. Their connection or lack thereof seems to define them.

I believe a core issue for human females is knowing that we have a reason to live and therefore we are valuable. Big Girls find that reason, whether they are single, married, divorced, or widowed. They recognize their value and go for the life God has promised. Others perpetually struggle, always looking for someone or something that is going to make them feel important. The truth is, we all struggle to find a sense of value and a reason to live. Some find these sooner than later, but if a girl is to emerge into the woman God created her to be, she will first have to discover and believe she is valuable and has a purpose.

Many women define themselves by the husband they marry and the children they raise. Now there are some real pitfalls with that perspective. Single Big Girls won't allow their lack of a mate and children to be the defining issue of their lives. Think of being single as having a layer of protective definition removed from your life. Imagine that you are forced to be known as Mary Jones, Single Woman, versus Mary Jones, Wife of John and Mother of Tim and Jennie. If you see yourself as "just" Mary Jones, you can wallow in self-pity, or you can begin to embrace several Big-Girl truths that will point you toward purposeful living:

- I do not need a significant other to be significant.

- I can have significant relationships with significant people.

- I enjoy my own company even though I also enjoy the company of others.

- I am responsible for my own happiness.

- Sometimes I have to work harder to make holidays and weekends special; but I do, and that's okay.

- I am not the only one who is single.

- I can enjoy being free to make choices for myself.

- I can be wise and seek counsel if I am in doubt about a decision I must make.

- I understand that "blood" is not required for a family kind of relationship with other people who are important to me.

- I avoid codependent entanglements that make me feel trapped or where I might trap another person.

- I believe in freedom.

Big-Girl singles understand that waiting for life to change will get them nowhere. Of course, that is the same for Big Girls in every situation. Singles in particular, however, must not wait and wait for an illusive partner to come along and share some kind of illusive tomorrow.

My friend Edna used to make me smile with her replies when people asked her when she was going to get married. One time she said, in response to the when-will-you-get-married question, "Oh, he died in the war." The person gulped and mumbled, "Oh, I'm sorry. I didn't know." Then Edna said, "He must have, he never showed up!" It was all I could do to keep from giggling out loud. Edna has a great perspective on life. She has lived as a fully functioning woman with great joy even though she is single. (Or maybe I should say *because* she is single.) She is elderly now and continues to be vibrant while living life to the max.

The principle truth that every Big Girl has to grab hold of, whether single, married, divorced, or widowed is this: You are valuable just because you are you. God has plans for you just because you are you. You came into the world alone, you will leave alone, and you will give an account—alone. The relationships you develop along your life's journey may be highly significant and part of God's plan, but they do not define you. You are precious by yourself and God is crazy about you. He hasn't left you beside the road of life to languish while you wait for something wonderful to happen or someone wonderful to come along. He has plans for you, just as you are, just where you are. So, if you are single and not very satisfied, shake off the "ho-hum mantle" and get on with it. Life is to be lived. Every day is part of your journey. Don't miss what God has for you.

PITFALLS FOR SINGLES

On your journey you will encounter pitfalls. Watch for them and remember, God has a bigger plan than all the earthly, petty stuff that seems to cloud our eyes and diminish our vision.

Codependency in friendships.

When I speak of codependency, I am speaking of the kind of relationship where one person negatively controls the emotions and behavior of another and vice versa.[1] This can happen to women who are not single, but it seems the single woman is particularly vulnerable to the codependency trap. I have seen very gifted, professional women reduced to bickering, crying, manipulation, and other Little-Girl behaviors because of codependency. Jealousy, control, and emotional dependency are manifestations of a Little Girl who would be so much happier if she learned to live as a Big Girl.

Usually, codependent singles are consumed with one relationship at a time, and when each one wears thin, they move to the next. If you were to get in such a woman's head and walk around, you would probably find the mind of a Little Girl who is very afraid that she will never have anyone to love her for being herself.

So she moves from one relationship to the other with an extreme dependency need, hoping to find the right person. She would like a man but often settles for a female "friend" who will be her all in all. It works for a while, but then it begins to crumble and eventually falls apart. Codependency is so very painful when the harvest of all that is planted in the dependent relationship begins to come in.

Maureen and Sharon had every reason to think of themselves as Big Girls. They were both successful in their careers, came from loving families, attended church, and professed the name of Jesus Christ. Since they were friends and were in their forties, they decided they could combine their finances, buy a home, and be more financially solvent if they owned a house together. They had never lived together or with anyone else, so they were understandably unaware of each other's baggage and the problems they might incur with the arrangement.

What Maureen didn't know was that Sharon was so frightfully insecure that she would take her as an emotional hostage before they had been in the house three months. Sharon began to read Maureen's mail, listen in on her phone conversations, and often follow her when she left the house just to see what she was doing. Maureen had no clue what she had done to bring out such bizarre behavior in Sharon. She just knew she felt paralyzed, stuck without hope of escape. That was Maureen's baggage and Little-Girl insecurity; Sharon's was fear that she would be abandoned.

I met these two at the height of their dysfunction. They felt trapped, desperate, and unable to find a solution. Maureen could talk about the situation, because she didn't want to continue to live as they were living. She just didn't know what to do. Sharon, on the other hand, was angry and hostile toward any outside intervention like counseling. She wanted the arrangement to work and for Maureen to just settle down and enjoy the situation. Maureen could not rest. Sharon could not let her fear go and let Maureen be herself. She decreed that Maureen must be a better friend, pay more attention to her and their friendship, and limit her contact with other friends. It was just that simple. If Maureen really cared about her, Sharon said, that is exactly what she should do.

When Maureen began to see the trap she was in, she made some major Big-Girl decisions, not the least of which was telling Sharon that she could not live in that kind of atmosphere, so she would be moving out the first of the month. As was expected, Sharon threw a Little-Girl fit, and over the next several months there seemed to be a war on that end of town. After several explosive encounters with Sharon, Maureen finally went on with her life. Maureen learned a very Big-Girl lesson from her blunder into that codependent relationship.

Sharon, on the other hand, met another woman who felt as needy as she felt. Within three months, Sharon had a new housemate, a new best friend, and was doing just fine, thank you. At the time I last heard of Sharon, she had been through several housemates and was looking for another one.

Codependency is a terrible trap for anyone, but for singles it can happen very quickly since there is no husband in the way. The door is wide open. That's the reason single Big Girls need to be vigilant for the signs of what could be a codependent trap:

- Telling too much too soon.
- Absence of healthy boundaries regarding personal identity and possessions.
- Proclaiming to be close too soon.

- Expectation that the other person will meet emotional needs, then anger when that doesn't happen.
- More pain than pleasure in the friendship.

Awareness is one of the marks of a Big Girl. So for the single Big Girl who is caught in an uncomfortable relationship where one or more of these behaviors is present, her antennae should be up. It's time to take the bull by the horns and do something. Staying put and being stagnant is not the way of the Big Girl. Instead, she takes responsibility for her own actions and then does what is healthy even if no one else understands. There will be many who do; they will be other Big Girls. But not everyone is a Big Girl. There will be many who don't understand. Little Girls who don't understand what it means to take responsibility and do something hard in a relationship will have a jaundiced view of what it takes to be responsible. They will be the ones who will say, "I can't believe you did that!" Or they will ask, "Don't you feel guilty for what has happened?" Little Girls are unaware of the big picture and have a hard time seeing it, even if you point it out. All they can see is what is right in front of them, today. As a result, you may encounter some of the following reactions to mature living from the Little Girls in your world.

- *Taking up the offense of another.* A Little Girl may get angry with you for taking a firm stand with a mutual acquaintance. She may feel honor bound to take the side of the other person.
- *Accusations and shaming.* She may accuse you of being insensitive or may say something like, "I can't believe you can live with yourself and act that way."

- *Bickering.* She may want to argue with you about your stand as a Big Girl.

- *The silent treatment.* She may just quit talking to you.

- *Group shunning.* The group you run around with may decide that you don't have much in common with them anymore. That happens when one person becomes a Big Girl and the group maintains their Little Girl ways. It just happens. It is nothing to worry about or even to try to talk about. No one will understand. You just have to know that there are Big Girls out there who will be your friends. Just keep going forward, and you will find them somewhere along the way. In the long run, you will be happier and healthier.

Allowing Too Much, Too Soon, Too Long in Dating

Mary Whelchel is a Big-Girl single friend of mine who was divorced many years ago and has remained single since. Mary is a straight shooter who has often spoken as a Big Girl to Little Girls who aren't quite sure of themselves and has given advice on how to become a Big Girl. She heads a great ministry to women called The Christian Working Woman and has written a very helpful book for singles called *Common Mistakes Singles Make.* I believe she has some insights that can really help singles in different areas of their lives. One area that has some particularly perilous pitfalls is dating. In her book, Mary identifies seven dating mistakes that create a good deal of tension in the life of a single woman. I have paraphrased each point below and then added my own thoughts on how they relate to Big-Girl singles.

1. Thinking you automatically understand the attentions of the opposite sex.

Don't assume anything when it comes to the attentions of a male. Assuming that you can read his signals (whatever they may be) will put you in a fragile, vulnerable place. You may be totally missing what he is really saying. A Big-Girl single knows to go with her head and not her heart until time has proven what the attentions are all about. It is easy to misinterpret when you want the outcome to be a certain way. I have talked with several women who were "sure" that the man they met really was interested but were devastated because he never called after the second or third meeting. That is an awful feeling that can be avoided by not assuming anything in the first place.

2. Believing that a bad relationship is better than no relationship.

A Little-Girl single's self-deception can be the worst. I have heard many of these women say, "I know he loves me," while they knew their boyfriend was seeing someone else. Being content with less than devoted attention and appreciation in a committed relationship is unacceptable to a Big-Girl single who knows who she is.

Game playing in which both parties are not totally honest makes for a rocky relationship. Putting up with less than the truth in your own heart or in his behavior will trip you up every time. I recently heard a sad story about someone who hung on too long to a bad relationship. She and her fiancé had parted ways over the issue of children: She wanted them; he didn't. He returned, begging for a reunion, claiming that he loved her so much he would have children to keep her. She believed him. After they married, he secretly had a vasectomy. Needless to say, their marriage disintegrated fast. This is the sad result of failing to pay attention to the pitfalls.

Hanging on too long just delays the inevitable and blocks your ability to move on. Once a relationship is obviously dead, bury it. Holding on, waiting for a broken dating relationship to repair itself is an exercise in futility.

3. Turning a blind eye to the red flags that pop up.

Most Little-Girl singles don't want to read danger signals such as frequent quarrels, obvious distancing, and unexplained absences. To read such signals for what they really indicate would mean that they have to change. A Little Girl often gets into relationships just to have a relationship. She does not believe she can be complete on her own. If there are warning signs, it is often easier for her to deny them than to deal with them, because having a relationship is more comfortable than being alone, which is too frightening. Instead, the Little-Girl single will often walk past the point of no return and then wonder why she always ends up in trouble.

4. Remaining naïve about physical temptations.^

Having the mistaken notion that they can control their emotions, Little-Girl singles are unaware of dangerous physical settings. Therefore, they see nothing wrong with being alone in compromising situations. Little-Girl singles don't sense that they could be in a difficult situation until they are in it. It would never occur to them to back out when the environment becomes a little too dark and a little too isolated. They don't acknowledge—or don't care—that there is great protection in group settings.

Big-Girl singles decide ahead of time exactly how far they will go and what they will do and with whom they will do it. God's standard is no sex outside of marriage. A Big Girl recognizes His rules are best even if her emotions are not that resolute. Given good thought processes ahead of time, a Big Girl will keep herself pure. Little Girls behave like God's standards don't exist, but His Word is very clear on this:

Do you not know that your bodies are members of Christ? Shall I then take away the members of Christ and make them members of a prostitute? May it never be! Or do you not know that the one who joins himself to a prostitute is one body with her? For He says, "THE TWO SHALL BECOME ONE FLESH." But the one who joins himself to the Lord is one spirit with Him. Flee immorality. Every other sin that a man commits is outside the body, but the immoral man sins against his own body. Or do you not know that your body is a temple of the Holy Spirit who is in you, whom you have from God, and that you are not your own? For you have been bought with a price: therefore glorify God in your body. (1 Corinthians 6:15–20)

When it comes down to a perilous moment in time when the lights are low and the opportunity for sex is available, there is no question for the Big Girl. She has made her decision ahead of time not to have sex outside of marriage. Of course, there is forgiveness for this sin, just as for any other, but sexual sin has such significant emotional ramifications that Big Girls don't want to have to deal with it. They will not hesitate to flee a tempting scenario.

5. Thinking that "Christian" automatically means "compatible."

Just because a guy claims to be a Christian and comes to the singles group carrying a Bible does not guarantee that he is marriageable material. In the enthusiasm of having found a Christian man, it is easy to look past the compatibility issue. It is also easy to look past whether he is truly a Christian or not. A man may say he is a Christian, but his word alone is not proof that he walks with God. Behavior over time is a good predictor of future behavior. Take time to get to know the man you believe is so wonderful. If he is God's man today, he will be God's man tomorrow and tomorrow and tomorrow. Don't rush into anything.

6. Evaluating men with a list of expectations they can't possibly meet.

Standing opposite women who expect too little are women who expect too much. It is easy to create a heady list of must-have qualities that even Superman could not live up to. Single Little Girls tend to be a little unrealistic about both themselves and their future mates. They each want a prince and assume he will get a princess in return. Our fallen nature pretty well eliminates that possibility in both cases. No princes and no princesses. We all are human, and that is what we have to deal with when we look for a mate. Big Girls have a realistic view of who they are and who would be marriageable material for them. Little Girls need to look at couples whose marriages they admire. Usually, the man and wife don't look like Ken and Barbie, and they don't live in a dream house with 2.4 children. Little Girls can become Big Girls by looking at others who have gone before and asking, "What do they have that I would like to have? What have they learned and how do they live in ways that appeal to me?"

I have a wonderful, artistic, creative friend who thought that she would be right only for artsy men. After several disappointments, she has come to the conclusion that she needs to be more realistic. A man who loves God and loves her is her only requirement now. It doesn't matter if he is a nuclear physicist, musician, or fireman. Her requirements are now different and more true to life. Her potential for marital happiness has gone up by a significant percentage.

7. Thinking that "alone" always means "lonely."

Sometimes Little Girls feel they can be okay only if there is someone else around, especially a man. Big-Girl singles enjoy their own company. They don't require the company of others to make their day. Getting to this place of comfort involves being okay with who you are. It doesn't mean that Big Girls don't get lonely, but they don't sit around and lament their loneliness. Instead, they look for ways to fill the void. They don't make life revolve around them. One of the best loneliness busters I know is to find someone who is lonelier or in need. Go to them, meet the need, and see how bad your loneliness is then.

ARE YOU WORRIED ABOUT MANY THINGS?

Wanting to grow and change is a desire that we all can embrace. The Lord loves His Big Girls, and He loves His Little Girls, too. He is forever using life lessons to keep us growing. These are great gifts. One of the best teaching illustrations for singles I know of is the story of Mary and Martha. I know, I know: Martha is in the kitchen, all in a dither over a meal, and Mary is sitting and listening to the rabbi. You may wonder what on earth this has to do with single Big Girls and Little Girls. Well, stick with me and let's step back in time to a house in Bethany in Israel. We'll pick up the story where the Bible does:

> Now it happened as they went that [Jesus] entered a certain village; and a certain woman named Martha welcomed Him into her house. And she had a sister called Mary, who also sat at Jesus' feet and heard His word. But Martha was distracted with much serving, and she approached Him and said, "Lord, do You not care that my sister has left me to serve alone? Therefore tell her to help me." And Jesus answered and said to her, "Martha, Martha, you are worried and troubled about

many things. But one thing is needed, and Mary has chosen
that good part, which will not be taken away from her." (Luke
10:38–42 NKJV)

There they are: four short, familiar verses, but as full of good
stuff for singles as for anyone else who cares to read them.

Martha, the single sister of single Mary and single Lazarus,
welcomed Jesus to her home and as you can well imagine, she went
about with great fanfare putting a meal on the table. She was
bustling about the kitchen when it occurred to her that Mary was
sitting around while there was work to be done. Believing that this
just wasn't right, Martha spoke with Jesus about this breach of
good behavior on Mary's part. Unruffled by her annoyance, Jesus
went to the heart of the whole problem, and it wasn't Mary. It was
what Martha was thinking. When He said, "Martha, Martha, you
are worried and troubled about many things," He was really saying
something much deeper than, "I am so sorry that you are in a tizzy
over the matzo balls." He was saying, "Martha, you have some
issues that you need to deal with." In fact, He was saying, "Martha,
you have a lot of things going on in your mind that are distracting
you from the most important thing, which Mary has chosen."

Whoa! Don't you know that Martha was blown away by that
comment? Here she thought she was really doing the right thing
for the Master and He tells her, "You missed it, and Mary has
found it."

THE SECRET OF MEANINGFUL SINGLEHOOD—
AND BEYOND

So what had Mary found? She had discovered the sweet truth that in
the grand scheme of things, only one thing really matters: a relation-

ship (living, breathing, vital, and real) with Jesus. She demonstrated her belief in this truth by sitting down when He was speaking. She didn't try to do two things at once, like keeping Martha happy in the kitchen while trying to listen to Jesus speaking in the other room. She made the very Big-Girl choice to sit at Jesus' feet and absorb everything He had to say. Martha, on the other hand, probably would have liked to sit there, but she had the notion that somehow she was responsible for everything that went on. There had to be a meal. That's all there was to it. It had to be served right then, no matter what was going on in the front room. After all, what would people say? What would people think? Those Little-Girl thoughts no doubt engulfed her as she huffed and puffed about the kitchen. Mary on the other hand, really didn't care. She just wanted to hear what Jesus had to say. She was the picture of calm and contentment, while Martha was the picture of confusion and consternation.

> **Big-Girl Truth to Live By:**
>
> *In the grand scheme of things, only one thing really matters: a relationship (living, breathing, vital, and real) with Jesus.*

Big Girls know a very special secret. It is the same secret that our brother Paul spoke about in the book of Philippians, when he wrote, "I have learned to be content in whatever circumstances I am" (Philippians 4:11). Contentment with the life you have been given is a choice. As you look at the big picture of life, Big Girls ask, what is most important here? What really matters? No matter what stage of life you are in, inevitably it all boils down to one truth: Your life is all about Christ and His work in it. Paul said it this way, "I know how to be abased, and I know how to abound.

Everywhere and in all things I have learned both to be full and to be hungry, both to abound and to suffer need. I can do all things through Christ who strengthens me" (Philippians 4:12–13 NKJV).

Making the choice to sit at Jesus' feet in every circumstance of life is foundational, key, to just about everything that it means to be a Big Girl. If all of us—single, married, widowed, divorced—would grab hold of this idea, we'd be on our way to Big Girlhood. Only when the truth of Jesus begins to penetrate our Little-Girl ways of thinking can we begin to grow.

There is a certain peace that comes when you realize that life is not all about you and what you can do. It is about who you are and what you can be as you! Because Big Girls find out who they are, they can do a lot of things well and with

> **Big-Girl Truth to Live By:**
>
> *No matter what stage of life you are in, your life is all about Christ and His work in it.*

good sense. After all is said and done, though, what matters is about the Big Girl within and who she is. Your true value is not about whom you married or didn't marry. It is not about how good you are at what you do. It is really just about one thing: What is your relationship to God? Have you made the decision to allow Him to call the shots? Have you decided to listen to Him and let Him comfort your soul? Have you given up your perceptions of how you think life should be? Have you accepted the fact that your life is in His hands and that He will enable you to do everything you need to do? Can you face each day with the confidence that you can do all things through Christ who strengthens you?

If so, my friend, you are among the Big Girls who are living with joy and contentment the life they have been given. If you can't say that yet, it's okay. You can start living that way today. Simply tell yourself, whatever is going on, "This is not about me. This is really all about Christ and His power to strengthen me and to get me through this day." That truth will get you through any stage of life, whether single or attached, whether young or old, whether sick or well. Christ is committed to you and longs for you to be committed to Him.

Oh, what a difference it makes when we give in and give up! You reach the point of living life with nothing to prove and nothing to lose. You can choose contentment and accept the sweet comfort of Christ's presence and provision for every step of the way.

Five

Wisdom for Big-Girl Wives

Becoming a Great Wife Who Has a Life

HE WAS ONLY GOING TO A SHAD BAKE, but I was in tears. Charlie and I had been married a few months, and we were living in a new town where he had work but we had no friends. The most exciting thing I did all day was walk two blocks downtown to buy the latest rage in soft drinks, a Fresca. We had a little two-room apartment in an old restored house, and I could only clean it so much. So when he came home and announced that he was going to a shad bake after work, I assumed that I would be going, too. When he said, "No wives will be there; it's just for the guys," everything within me melted into a very sad, disappointed Little Girl, and I did what a Little Girl would do in that situation: I cried! I couldn't believe that he would go to such an event without me. Why wouldn't he forego it to stay home with me, if I couldn't go? Why didn't he care?

Of course, now I look back on that moment and smile. I was a Little Girl wife who needed to grow up and come to the realization that my husband was not responsible for my happiness. He did not have to save me from my loneliness or my self-pity. It just wasn't his job. I was responsible for me. That is a tough truth to grasp, but it was a major step for me toward becoming a Big-Girl wife. I had married under the mistaken notion that Charlie would be everything to me. He would lead me, take care of me, be my husband, my lover, the father of my children, my provider, and my friend. I, on the other hand, would be his lover, wife, mother of his children, and friend. It never crossed my mind in those early years that I had responsibility for myself. It never occurred to me that I was responsible for my own emotional well-being, my spiritual development, and my physical wellness. I believed that somehow it would just work out because we loved each other. Love is a good start, but there is more to this Big-Girl marriage thing than just loving each other and being one another's all in all.

Each partner in a marriage has a role to play. When you begin to embrace your own role and the truth of personal responsibility and fulfillment, you will take a huge amount of pressure off of your relationship.

No Man Can Do It All

Many couples start their marriages under an extreme patriarchal system, where the husband is totally responsible for his wife's well-being, physically, emotionally, and spiritually. But that kind of setup doesn't hold up well under the stresses of life and the demands of a growing family. When God created woman and instituted marriage, He said, "It is not good (sufficient, satisfactory) that the man should be alone; I will make him a helper meet (suitable, adapted, complementary) for him" (Genesis 2:18 AMP). That does not sound to me like a Little-Girl wife who must be cared for physically, emotionally, and spiritually. It sounds as if the man and the woman are to be complementary of one another: Where he is weak, she can be strong, and vice versa.

A wife is given to the man to complete him, not to compete with him. If she is going to be a completer, then she needs to recognize her own competency and insights that she brings to the table. A Big Girl understands that men and women are different, and she celebrates those differences. She doesn't expect her husband to know everything about everything any more than she should know everything about everything. A Big Girl believes that she can be one of the best assets her husband has, and she works to be just that. She also gives credit to assets of his that enhance her life, but she doesn't put him on a pedestal where he will heroically solve all of her problems. That is a formula for pure disaster. Neither does she view him as an incompetent who would be nothing with out her.

Marriage was never meant for children, but for two adults who recognize that they are different; therefore, their roles are different. A woman who sees herself as a Little Girl can never fully succeed in her role. She will forever be looking to her husband for her happiness. Her husband won't be able to succeed either when forced to play the roles of both husband and father to his Little-Girl wife. No man can.

A father is responsible for his little girl's mental, physical, and emotional well-being. He also is responsible to correct her and guide her character formation. He eventually will have to let her go. A husband, on the other hand, is called to love his wife sacrificially, but he doesn't have to make sure she gets to bed on time, does her chores well, and acts nice at the grocery store. These are her responsibilities. In fact, if he believes that he is responsible to make sure his wife does these things, he probably will end up with either a helpless Little-Girl wife or a very offended Big Girl who won't stand for such treatment.

Bud and Lynn learned this lesson too late. They started out their life together with Bud being the controlling, always-in-charge, fingers-in-every-pie kind of guy. Lynn looked to him for her care and keeping. It seemed like a good setup, because Bud loved Lynn and Lynn loved Bud. They were good to each other, and Lynn was perfectly satisfied to look to Bud for everything in her life. He was her all in all. Bud loved being the answer man for Lynn. So the whole thing worked—for a while.

Then the children began to come. One by one their tribe increased, and Bud couldn't cover all of the expected bases. He couldn't be the provider and the emotional nurturer that he and Lynn assumed he should be. He worked overtime trying to make everyone happy. He tried to play with his kids every night as well as sit and listen to Lynn tell him about her day. Lynn very often was overwhelmed with the antics of the children and saw herself as not quite capable of handling them. She wanted Bud to take over the children after he came home from work. After all, they were his as well as hers, and she just couldn't cope. She often dissolved in tears or resorted to tantrums to get the message across that she was needy.

Bud, however, needed Lynn to be his completer. He didn't need a Little Girl running to him with her frustrations, expecting him to be her daddy who would make everything okay. While Bud was facing the fact that he had a wife as needy as his three toddlers, Lynn decided that the answer to her frustrations was that Bud needed to be more involved. He tried but could never quite get it right for Lynn. The tension built between them. Bud stayed away from home and worked more. Lynn cried more and blamed Bud for her sadness. Bud worked more. Lynn cried more. The children lived in a sad house while Bud and Lynn's lopsided world crumbled around them. After several years of this tension, they didn't have anything in common left but the children, who just seemed to be in the way. It was a sad day when Bud walked out and said, "I'll send you my paycheck, but, Lynn, I have nothing more to give." He could no longer be a daddy both to his children and his Little-Girl wife. Her needs seemed to be limitless, and he could not go on.

IMITATE THE PORTRAIT OF A BIG-GIRL WIFE

I haven't always felt so kindly toward Proverbs 31, which seemed like one big housekeeping job the first time I read it. But over the years I have come to understand and appreciate the life of the woman described in this chapter of the Word. If you have assumed that she is an overworked, obsessive-compulsive housewife, you might take another look. She is a safe Big Girl who knows her abilities, fulfills her role, and is a blessing to her family. We don't know if her husband was everything she would have liked him to be, but we do know that she knew her role, and she performed it well. She knew how to be a Big Girl in any situation. In her, we wives have a picture of the potential for our side of marriage. This is the part we can do something about! Remember, Big-Girl wives look for what they can do about their situation. They don't flail around waiting for Prince Charming to come charging in to make everything all right.

The woman described in Proverbs 31 was the kind of woman King Lemuel's mother wanted him to have, albeit he may not have wanted this kind of woman. Young men often believe that a sexy, dependent Little Girl will make a great wife. Tunnel vision makes a kittenish girl look like a great life partner. The long view of a life already lived will refute that thinking in a heartbeat. King Lemuel's mother knew it. She told her boy, "Give not your strength to [loose] women, nor your ways to those who and that which ruin and destroy kings" (Proverbs 31:3 AMP). A woman doesn't have to be "loose" to destroy a marriage. A Little Girl like Lynn can sap a husband's strength and cause him to miss what their lives together could have been had they both been grown up.

I like Lemuel's mother. She had a good, Big-Girl head on her shoulders, and she obviously knew her son and what he would need in a wife to succeed. She wanted her son to take a wife who would be a blessing not only to him but to herself and to her children as well. That's how marriage works the very best. Look for a woman who is capable, intelligent, and virtuous, she told her son. Talk about a treasure: Lemuel's mother said this kind of woman is far above rubies or pearls (v. 10 AMP), trustworthy (v. 11), and always good to her husband (v. 12). "Son," King Lemuel's mother might have said, "listen when I tell you the kind of woman who will make a good wife."

She does her husband only good for as long as she lives. "The heart of her husband trusts in her confidently and relies on and believes in her securely, so that he has no lack of [honest] gain or need of [dishonest] spoil. She comforts, encourages, and does him only good as long as there is life within her" (31:11–12 AMP). A Big-Girl wife can afford to serve like that because she isn't always caught up in the Me Syndrome. She knows that to do her best in loving her husband and her children is best for her. She isn't diminished by serving them; she is made stronger. This is the heart of the Big Girl.

She wants to do a good job and be trustworthy. She isn't always waiting for her husband to become the paragon of virtue that he should be. The Big-Girl wife is trustworthy even when her mate may not be. That's a hard pill to swallow, but the opposite happens more often than we would like to admit: "He's not trustworthy; why should I be?" Or, "Well, if he will be such and so, *then* I will too." If you wait for your husband to do whatever it is that you think he should do, you may wait a long time and settle for less than God has for you.

What do you do if you find yourself married to a man who has betrayed your confidence? Run? Stay miserable and wait for him to change? Pout, hoping that someone will notice? None of that works. However tough your situation, you can be the one who is just fine in the middle of it.

I recently met Sheila, who had the demeanor of a woman at peace. She was quietly radiant. She had married a good man, but he did not share her faith in God. She knew that she had bitten off a lot to chew, because as she matured, her faith became more and more important to her. She has learned how to embrace the secret of contentment. "I have learned that when my expectations of Rob become bigger than the possibility of his fulfilling them, I have to turn to the truth found in Philippians 4:11–13:

> I have learned how to be content (satisfied to the point where I am not disturbed or disquieted) in whatever state I am. I know how to be abased and live humbly in straitened circumstances, and I know also how to enjoy plenty and live in abundance. I have learned in any and all circumstances the secret of facing every situation, whether well-fed or going hungry, having a sufficiency and enough to spare or going without and being in want. I have strength for all things in Christ Who empowers me [I am ready for anything and equal to anything through Him Who infuses inner strength into me; I am self-sufficient in Christ's sufficiency] (AMP).

Rob is a handful, but Sheila is able to be all right because she has come to the glorious realization that Rob is not the source of her happiness, her strength, or her well-being. He is her husband, not her father. Nor is he her Little-Boy husband. He is not her kid to care for. He is not dependent on her, always looking to her for assurance that he is really an okay person. I've met quite a few Little-Boy husbands. They like the perks of marriage, but they like having a wife who, like their mother, solves all of their problems, too. So a Big-Girl wife doesn't have to look to her husband to solve her problems, nor does she have to take care of him so that he won't face the problems of the world. She has learned to be "self-sufficient in Christ's sufficiency."

Being "self-sufficient in Christ's sufficiency" means being at peace with God, yourself, and your mate by allowing Christ to be the answer to your questions. A Big Girl doesn't look for answers in her mate. She doesn't expect him to be the superhuman provider of her stability or her sanity or her peace. She recognizes that Christ is the power within her to deal with whatever she comes up against. It doesn't take a wife very long to realize that her husband cannot always be there for some of the "oh wow, what now?" times in her life.

Charlie and I raised three boys. Whenever I had to run to the doctor with busted chins or fingers that had been slammed in car doors or hands that had fishhooks stuck in them, he was never there. That wasn't by design but by circumstance. Charlie was often on military duty or working out of town, and he just wasn't available. It always fell to me to get the boys to the ER by myself. I really never gave it a thought at the time. I just did what mothers do: I took care of the kids. It was only after the boys left home that it occurred to me, *I don't believe Charlie ever made it to the ER or doctor's office with the boys.* Through all of those years (the boys are in their thirties now), I learned the secret of being self-sufficient in Christ. That is, I learned that I could do what needed to be done and be what I needed to be *because I had Christ living in me giving me the strength and wisdom I needed to get the job done.* That is why it is possible to say, "I can do all things through Christ who strengthens me."

Once that is settled in your own mind and you are firmly convinced that it is true, you can turn your heart and head toward living life as a Big-Girl wife who does her job well. Give up waiting for your husband to become what you want him to be or to show up when you think you need him. On some days it may not seem possible, but you can grab hold of what you can be and then go for it. You will find that you are more productive and peaceful as you live out your role as a wife!

Now back to the list from King Lemuel's mother:

She adds to the family income whenever she can. "She considers a [new] field before she buys or accepts it [expanding prudently and not courting neglect of her present duties by assuming other duties]; with her savings [of time and strength] she plants fruitful vines in her vineyard" (Proverbs 31:16 AMP). "Lemuel," Mom says, "this will be a good woman for you."

She understands the laws of spiritual, mental, and physical health, and she obeys them. "She girds herself with strength [spiritual, mental, and physical fitness for her God-given task] and makes her arms strong and firm" (v. 17 AMP). "Lemuel, you will need this kind of strength in a woman."

She can be counted on to be there through the hard times as well as the good. "She tastes and sees that her gain from work [with and for God] is good; her lamp goes not out, but it burns on continually through the night [of trouble, privation, or sorrow, warning away fear, doubt, and distrust" (v. 18 AMP). "Lemuel, she is faithful and tenacious."

She is a giver. "She opens her hand to the poor, yes, she reaches out her filled hands to the needy [whether in body, mind, or spirit]" (v. 20 AMP). "And Lemuel, she is so strong."

She is not fearful of days to come. She lives well the days given.
"Strength and dignity are her clothing, and her position is strong
and secure; she rejoices over the future [the latter day or time to
come, knowing that she and her family are in readiness for it]!"
(v. 25 AMP). "Lem, you will love the peace this woman brings to
your home!"

*She is wise and respected by those who know her best—her children,
and her husband.* "She opens her mouth in skillful and godly
Wisdom, and on her tongue is the law of kindness [giving counsel
and instruction]. She looks well to how things go in her household, and the bread of idleness (gossip, discontent, and self-pity)
she will not eat. Her children rise up and call her blessed (happy,
fortunate, and to be envied); and her hus-
band boasts of and praises her, [saying], . . .
Charm and grace are deceptive, and beauty
is vain [because it is not lasting], but a
woman who reverently and worshipfully fears the Lord, she shall
be praised! Give her of the fruit of her hands, and let her own
works praise her in the gates [of the city]!" (vv. 26–31 AMP).

> **Big-Girl Truth to Live By:**
>
> *Big Girls don't have to have every-
> thing perfect to be okay.*

This is some kind of woman. Lemuel's mother knew the kind
of woman that brings completion to any man, and that is what she
wanted for her boy.

As a Big-Girl wife, you can do and be what God wants no
matter what your mate may be like. This may sound very airy, but
Big Girls recognize that even when they are married, they have
options. Remember that's a key difference between children and
adults: Children have no options; adults do. Children can't make

choices about the way they are treated; adults can. Circumstances don't have to be perfect, and a husband's behavior doesn't have to qualify for being wonderful for a Big-Girl wife to choose to be okay and to get on with her life. One of my favorite Big-Girl statements is, "We do things in spite of, not because of." Big Girls don't have to have everything perfect to be okay.

BIG-GIRL WIVES DON'T STICK AROUND FOR ABUSE

Now, let me say right here that I do not think it is wise to try to be a Big Girl in the household with an abusive mate. By "abusive" I am speaking of someone who physically or mentally beats you. First of all, it won't work. An abuser's greatest goal is to tear you down and to make you subservient. If he fails in that, he will only redouble his efforts, because keeping you small is the only way he can feel important.

If you try to live the life of a Big Girl with an abuser you will only be assaulted that much more. You have to leave an abuser to be able to live life as a Big Girl. I want to encourage you: If you are living with an abuser, the Big-Girl wife thing to do is to leave him with his own stuff. I am not talking divorce. I'm saying move out. Let the consequences of his behavior fall in around him. Most of the time, abusers blame everyone but themselves for their unhappiness and discontent. They don't see how they could possibly be the problem when they can make their spouse the target of their anger. A Big Girl who leaves removes her husband's whipping girl from the equation. She also removes his excuse for the way he behaves. Leaving him makes him face his stuff. No self-respecting Big Girl will stay in a place where she is berated, beaten, and dumped like baggage on the side of the road. A Big Girl takes responsibility for herself and takes care of herself. She will not allow anyone, even a husband, to continue to abuse her.

I know there are those who have encouraged women to stay in abusive situations while they wait on God to do a miracle. I don't see that in Scripture. God can do miracles while you are in a safe place just as well as He can while you sit in danger never knowing what will happen next. If you believe that getting out is the course you need to take, it is important to enlist help. Trusted friends can encourage you and be there for you. It is usually best not to go to one of their homes, because an abuser will often turn his wrath on your friends. Most cities of any size have safe havens for women who are in abusive situations; check your Yellow Pages. If you are going to leave, it is important that you prepare to do it quickly and with a few supplies. Pack extra clothing for you and the children, put back enough money for a motel room if you should need it, and have an extra set of keys made. Then, when the time is right, leave.

One of my greatest frustrations in counseling has been working with women who say they want to be Big Girls but don't stay the course. They don't want to live in their abusive marriages anymore, and some even muster up the courage to leave. They try it for a while, but then when the going gets tough, they choose to return to the situation rather than facing life as a Big Girl.

This is tragic, because severe consequences can follow a woman who abdicates her Big-Girl role. When it comes to volatile situations, things can get out of control quickly.

I heard about a family that was torn apart because of the abusive, childish behavior of the husband and his wife. They had some serious marital conflicts, but instead of dealing with them by separating or getting good counseling help, they continued to live together in strife. They kept their issues to themselves for years.

People around them knew there were problems, but the couple always managed to get back on an even keel and go on with life.

The wife went to her family home for a visit one summer and began to talk to her brothers about the marital difficulties she and her husband had been having. Once she began talking, she didn't stop. She intimated that sometimes she was afraid of her husband because he raged at her. Her brothers were hotheads and took it upon themselves to "do something about it." Believing they could terrify their brother-in-law into behaving, they took a gun and went to his house. Instead of just frightening him, an argument ensued and they shot him. Unfortunately, he died.

When his wife found out what had happened, she was shocked. She didn't mean for him to be killed. She didn't mean for her children to be without a father. She didn't mean for her brothers to go to prison. She didn't mean, she didn't mean . . . But the sad truth is, she could have done more than she did to prevent the whole dismal affair if she had taken control of the situation early on and gotten help. Living separately until he got serious counsel was an option. Or if he refused counsel, living apart and using the law to restrain him if he came around would have been another option. The problem is, she saw herself as helpless, and she didn't want to make waves in her marriage. What she failed to see was that the waves were getting higher and higher, and she needed to find a way to get her boat to shore before it capsized, but she didn't. Now, she's drowning in a sea of sorrow that didn't have to be.

Once we become physical adults, we have to parent ourselves. We become responsible for our choices and for the consequences of those choices. No longer can we look to another human being to parent us. We make the decisions and we deal with the results. I believe many women have been misguided in this point by well-meaning teachers and preachers who have taught women that husbands are their umbrella, or covering. Where is it written? While it is true in God's order of things—the man is ultimately responsible for his submission to God and his treatment of his wife and children—this responsibility does not in any way make his wife any less responsible for *her* behavior or *her* choices.

A wife is responsible to revere her husband, just as he is called upon to love her. If she submits to him and he is wrong, then she is still responsible for her submission. He will bear responsibility, but she will not be set free from the fallout. The same consequences will come to her whether she makes a poor choice with or without her husband's guidance. Poor choices usually end in poor results. That's the law of the universe. It is naïve to think that if you submit to what is wrong God will make it right.

Now, for all those who love Him, God does promise He will cause all things to work together for good (Romans 8:28), but why put God in the position of making some disaster work together for good when it could have been avoided with some Big-Girl wisdom? We will never make all the right choices. Wrong choices are unavoidable, especially when we don't know all the facts. But when we know the facts and nevertheless go against what is right in the name of following our husband, there is something wrong.

I heard a blatant illustration of this on a tape several years ago. A woman was teaching on a perfectly good, biblical word: submission—teaching that mindless submission is fraught with peril. This woman told a story about her husband's treatment of her little boy. The child had been put to bed and kept getting up. The rest of the family, which included two older daughters, were having dinner together. The little boy kept being sent back to bed. When he came out of the bedroom about the fourth time, the father jumped up from the table and ran after him, yelling at the top of his lungs. The little boy, of course, ran back to his room crying. His sisters were indignant and complained to their mother that their father's behavior had been frightening. The mother told them that the father was the head of the household and that they were all to submit to his authority because that was the way they would have to submit to their husbands. The father returned to the table to eat. The little boy continued to cry in his bedroom, and the two girls learned a warped lesson about submission.

Going along with bad behavior is not submission. If a wife is a completer, then when her husband bounds out of line, she is well within the responsibility of her role to mention that he might want to think of another way to do something. Again, to mindlessly follow is just that, mindless. Big Girls avoid being mindless, even if their moves are not popular.

At the same time, Big Girls also avoid nagging and taking on the demeanor of self-willed Little Girls. They are reasonable and are willing to submit to their husband's sound leadership even if it is not their favorite thing to do. They don't have to have their way about everything and can be reasoned with. Big Girls understand that the whole heart of biblical submission is about fitting in with their mates, working together with them, and sticking together like glue. Little-Girl wives, on the other hand, soon tire of having to think about fitting in with husbands. They are easily frustrated and angered and can make life miserable for husbands who are trying to lead as they should.

Big-Girl Wives Help Little-Boy Husbands Mature

I was in a phone store this week and saw a perfect illustration of a Big-Girl wife having to deal with a Little-Boy husband. The lines were long and the wait was tedious. The wife stood in line to receive service while her husband went from one phone to the other on display and played with the bells and whistles. He set off all of the ringers, stepping on every last nerve of the people in line. His wife, who happened to be very pregnant, finally made the comment to no one in particular, "He's like this all the time, one big kid." He seemed nice enough, just immature and unaware of what was going on around him.

Dealing with a Little-Boy husband requires a special skill. Trying to make him grow up isn't the answer. Fussing at him isn't the answer. Being cold isn't the answer, yet I can see how one would want to do all of those things. It has to be frustrating when you "get it" but live with someone who doesn't. But God didn't say that if you marry a Little Boy, you can go ahead and bail out on him. Big Girls know that love and kindness go a long way toward drawing another person toward a more mature life.

This is where being secure in yourself and in your relationship with the Lord can take you a long way. It's applicable whether your husband is a Little Boy, a grump, distant, or a man with whom you discover you have little in common. Love still covers a multitude of sins, and to a great degree that is what marriage is about, especially when you realize you haven't married the man you wanted or thought you had. When you recognize that you are different, your thought life becomes very significant. Remember, Big Girls don't dwell on the minors. They home in on the majors, and that is where they camp. Even Little-Boy husbands, grumpy husbands, or distant husbands all have some good qualities that you can focus your thoughts on. It is an amazing thing: When you think on the characteristics that are good in your mate and are grateful for those qualities, you will find you can tolerate the other things he does with a much better humor.

BIG-GIRL WIVES DON'T PLAY WORD GAMES

A Big-Girl wife doesn't play emotional games with her husband. She uses words to communicate. She doesn't resort to "The Guessing Game," to test him and his love for her. She doesn't proudly announce, "Well if I have to tell you what I want, that takes the joy out of it." If you are a smart Big Girl, you will know that you have to open your mouth and say what you want. Your husband is not tele-pathic. A Big-Girl wife tries to speak in terms that she and her husband will understand so there is no misunder-standing. This takes work, patience, trial

> **Big-Girl Truth to Live By:**
>
> *You have to open your mouth and say what you want. Your husband is not telepathic.*

and error, and prayer. This is true whether she is dealing with a difficult issue between them or whether she is explaining how the dishwasher overflowed.

Words are so very important and are to be handled with great care. Big-Girl wives know this and are careful in the way they speak. If you are caught up in a childish discussion, it is so easy for it to degenerate to a childish skirmish. Yelling, screaming, sarcasm, and low-blow remarks need to be left to the children. A Big-Girl wife doesn't stoop to that kind of conversation, even though she may be talking with a Little-Boy husband who wants to react that way.

A Big Girl can control the tone of her conversation even though her partner doesn't. That's one of the great things about being a Big Girl. You can choose your reactions. You can choose what you think.

You can choose what you feel. You can choose how you respond. That sounds pretty cut and dried, but once you realize you have that kind of power and personal control, it really gives you a confidence that is quite wonderful. That doesn't mean that remarks can't hurt or that you are not taken aback by what your mate might say to you, but you can determine how long you plan to nurse the hurt.

One Big-Girl question you can ask is, "When you said thus and such, did you want me to feel rejected?" or, "When you made the comment about _____, did you mean for me to feel totally defeated?" Then you can add, "Because right now that is what I am feeling." Then wait for the answer. If it is, "Oh, no," then you can ask, "Then what were you trying to communicate?" If the answer is, "Yes, that's what I meant," then you have to accept it and decide what to do with it. At least you have clarified the issue and don't have to spend unnecessary time wondering what is really going on. It also gives your mate a chance to recant some hotheaded comment that he really didn't mean. If he says, "How on earth did you get that out of what I said?" then it might be good to point out the words, body language, gestures, or whatever it was that made you "get that" out of what he said. He may want to continue the discussion over *how* he said something, but always try to bring it back to the problem that launched the conversation in the first place.

Communication is hard work. You can be married for decades and still wonder if you are really communicating, but don't give up. Big Girls want to communicate and are willing to do the hard work to do it well.

A Big-Girl Wife Is a Treasure

A Big-Girl wife brings richness to the marriage, and although it may be stormy from time to time, in the end, her stability and wisdom will have been a significant calming force that helped the relationship work. It is her job, after all, to be her husband's completer. If she does it well, she truly is more valuable than any earthly riches. Many marriages are intact today because a wife decided to be a Big Girl when things got tough and the road became steep. On the other hand, many children are safe today and feel secure because a Big-Girl wife and mother said, "No more."

It is not the circumstances that determine the designation of Big-Girl wife. It is the Big-Girl wife who determines how she will handle the circumstances. That is what makes her a treasure!

Six

Savvy for Big-Girl Moms

Finding the Solutions Every Real Mom Needs

WHEN ONE OF MY BOYS WAS SIX, he broke the glass top of a coffee table we had in our living room. He didn't mean to break it, but the deed was done. I was put out with him because he had been goofing off when the accident happened. I scolded him and sent him to his room while I cleaned up the glass. With that chore out of the way, I went to the bedroom to continue the scolding. (I know, I know. Enough is enough, but it is what I did.) He was lying on his bunk bed trying to get over his tears. I fussed at him about how irresponsible he had been, and in the heat of my comments I rashly said, "You are going to have to pay for this!" Still snuffling and crying he said, "But I'm only a little boy and I don't have a job." At that moment, I snapped to and realized that I was the Big-Girl mommy and he was truly just a little boy. I didn't need to heap my frustrations on him, but for a split second I forgot who was the adult.

If I have any regrets about being the parent of my three sons, I guess it would be that I wasn't a Big-Girl mom from the beginning.

In many ways I feel as if I was just a child when they were born, and we all grew up together. I'm grateful that we all survived pretty well intact, but it was not because I acted like a Big Girl all of the time. Only the grace of God and our ability as a family to forgive each other and get on with life kept us whole.

The beauty of children is that they have a lot of resilience in the face of our grown-up mistakes. For this we all can be grateful. If I'd had some Big-Girl mom skills, however, perhaps I could have headed off some of the struggles we did experience! A Little-Girl mom can do a lot of damage even though her children are resilient. Their ability to bounce back can get used up if their mother's girlishness is relentless. A Little-Girl mom is very self-absorbed. Her children make her feel good or bad about herself, depending on how they act or react. Little-Girl moms, for example, put a lot of emphasis on how their children make them look. As a result, they can be too strict and demand too much from little hands and little minds. Other Little-Girl moms are just the opposite; they let their children go wild, never acknowledging that other people might be bothered by their children's antics. A Big-Girl mom operates somewhere between these two extremes. She knows how to curtail her children appropriately, but she knows how to give them enough freedom to grow and explore without her hovering over them.

A Big-Girl mom knows that the big picture of motherhood is not about her children's behavior, nor is it about her. The big picture is about her heart for God and her desire for her children to find a vital relationship with Him. Accomplishing that requires a mature wisdom on her part that governs how she relates to her children. A Big-Girl mom knows that relationship is the most important issue she will deal with, because when her children are grown, no matter what path they choose to walk, she wants a relationship with them.

Principles for Big-Girl Moms of Young Children

Like God, good earthly parents always desire relationship with their children. Big-Girl moms know that healthy relationships are nourished by boundaries. You can't have relationship without a plan for healthy relating. Little-Girl moms focus on the relationship right now, with no view toward future relating. Her attention is on nothing but the moment and immediate convenience. Big Girls understand that a longer view is in order.

> **Big-Girl Truth to Live By:**
>
> *Healthy relationships are nourished by boundaries. You can't have relationship without a plan for healthy relating.*

When you are establishing your Big-Girl parenting style, there are some principles you will need to embrace and remember in order to keep the boundaries for healthy relating in place. A parenting style is the way you and your spouse have determined to work with your children to bring them into maturity. The following truths are principles that I consider essential to Big-Girl parenting. You might think about adding them to your parenting philosophy as you consider how to best raise your precious little ones.

Parenting Is Not About You

When you are a Big Girl, parenting is not about you, your anger, or your childhood issues. It is not about what you don't like in your child, yourself, or your husband. It is about your child's welfare, his success as a human being, and his obedience to what is right. I think one of the great shocks to Little Girls when they become moms is that they discover life isn't about them anymore. It is about their children and their children's needs. Their instinct is to deny this. Accepting this truth is a real growing curve and often marks the point where a Little-Girl mom moves into the ranks of Big-Girl moms. The transformation may take awhile, but it can happen with a little awareness.

I remember a great growth spurt that happened with me when I was twenty-three years old. It was the middle of the night. I had a screaming baby on my shoulder. As I passed by the bathroom mirror on the way to the changing table, I saw myself holding this child. I was exhausted, but in that moment it occurred to me: "This is my child, and I am his mother." I had a lot of growing to do, but it started in that moment of revelation. That which is obvious sometimes has to be revealed. With that fleeting glance in the mirror, my responsibility was revealed to me that night. I would be responsible, very responsible, for a long time, and then I would have to let go.

Letting go is something we can do only when we realize parenting is not about us. In the first chapter of 1 Samuel we can read the story of Hannah, who longed for a son more than anything else in the world. Her husband did not understand the depth of her pain, and his second (fertile) wife taunted her. But Hannah persisted in asking God for a son and made Him a vow:

> Oh, GOD-of-the-Angel-Armies,
> If you'll take a good, hard look at my pain,
> If you'll quit neglecting me and go into action for me
> By giving me a son,
> I'll give him completely, unreservedly to you.

I'll set him apart for a life of holy discipline.
(1 Samuel 1:11 MSG)

Within a year she gave birth to Samuel. She cradled him in her arms and remembered her vow. Now I don't know about you, but it's hard to imagine wanting a baby as badly as Hannah did and then knowing she would have to give him up one day soon! But she kept her word without wavering. When Samuel was weaned, she took him to live with Eli the priest. Hannah did a very Big-Girl thing. She knew that Samuel did not come into this world for her, but for God. He belonged to the Lord. She gave Samuel back to Him.

Imagine how much harder this was, considering the circumstances: Hannah would see Samuel only once a year when she and her husband went to the tabernacle for the yearly sacrifice. She didn't know whether her arms would ever know the tender hug of a child again. Hannah knew her boy would live in a household with an old priest and his two decadent sons. Surely her mother heart cried out with questions for the Lord: "I know I gave him to You, Lord, but these conditions are deplorable. Those boys of Eli are so rough and ungodly. My little boy is dedicated to You!"

But Hannah did not go back on her promise. She said, "I prayed for this child, and GOD gave me what I asked for. And now I have dedicated him to GOD. He's dedicated to GOD for life" (1 Samuel 1:27–28 MSG).

God took care of Samuel, and He blessed Hannah with three more sons and two daughters! Samuel grew to be a judge of Israel, a prophet, and a priest. I know plenty of young moms who worry about sending their children out into the world, but that is what God asks us to do, isn't it? Because parenting is not about us, but about partnering with God to prepare our kids—future Big Girls and Boys—to do His work.

UNDER ROOF, UNDER RULE

If your child lives under your roof, then your rules apply to that child's life. If your child leaves your roof (and by my definition that means he also leaves your financial input into his life) then he is no longer under your rules. What could be clearer? If you can establish this principle when your children are toddlers, it will be easier to toe the line when they become teenagers. They will recognize that you are a Big-Girl mom who has taken her rightful place of authority alongside Dad, if he is in the home. They will know almost instinctively, if you have been at this since childhood, that it is good and proper for parents to have authority and for children to obey. It is God's plan. "Children, obey your parents in everything, for this pleases the Lord" (Colossians 3:20 NIV). Of course, this doesn't mean that they won't buck against authority, but you have set the standard so they know what is expected.

BOUNDARIES ARE NECESSARY; LEASHES ARE NOT

Big-Girl moms understand the value of building fences and avoiding leashes. Fences are those wonderful boundaries that keep children safe while giving them room to play. Leashes, on the other hand, are restrictive tethers that keep the parent and the child tied to one another. Neither one has the space they need to function well.

When I was young and newly married, my husband and I lived in a mobile-home park in a college town. The young couple that lived in the next trailer had a leash for their toddler son so he could be outside and they wouldn't have to worry about him wandering off. It was adequate for his safety, but it always bothered me to see him confined like that. The tether gave him about three feet of play space. I don't suppose there was a law against it, but a yard with space to play and sturdy fences would have been preferable. That's what fence boundaries are about. They give plenty of space to explore with lots of security. When used properly, boundaries are understood by parent and child alike and give security to both of them.

When our boys were toddlers, Charlie and I determined that we wanted strong boundaries for behaviors that could be disruptive or disrespectful. That was where we drew the limits with our boys. We wanted them to "live free" until it came to invading someone else's space or being sassy. Those were two things that we would not tolerate under any circumstances. Even through their teenage years, these rules remained. Our good relationship was fenced by mutual respect that forbade disruptive or disrespectful behavior. If it occurred, we dealt with it swiftly, cleared the air, and got back to the business at hand.

Establishing healthy boundaries starts early with the simple task of putting up gates to confine toddlers to a safe play area. The process then evolves to moving your boundaries out little by little until, at last, your child is grown and responsible for her own behavior. As your child grows, you loosen your control. Age-appropriate discipline and character development are what the process is about. As you see your little girl becoming more and more responsible, you can let go a little bit more of your responsibility.

I have three granddaughters, ages six years, three years, and six months. (I have two grandsons as well, but for the sake of illustration, I'll use the girls.) Each of them has boundaries at my house that are weighted toward their ages and abilities. Lauren, the six-year-old is reliable. So I don't keep checking the door to the pool to see if she has slipped out there. I have loosened my boundaries with her. Rachel is three. She thinks doors are to be opened and anywhere she goes is all right. Clearly, I have much tighter reins on her. When she is at my house, my ears are tuned to every sound, and I don't let her out of my sight. Rebekah is six months old. She can't go far, but she can roll over. For now, I am super-careful about where I put her down, making sure she is not in danger of falling from a high place. She is totally dependent, so I watch her carefully for things she might put into her mouth or for pillows and corners she might wriggle into. Although my boundaries for each of them vary according to their ages, I have one goal in mind as their Big-Girl grandmother: I want them to grow up to be healthy, self-contained, and able to live independently as mature women. I know it all starts with those little boundaries that will be loosened every year. These girls will grow, guided by boundaries, all the way from babyhood through their teen years and until they are independent and on their own. By that time, parenting goals for training a self-governing Big Girl will be achieved—or at least they will be out of the house!

CONSISTENCY MATTERS

When a Big-Girl mom is faced with the job or rearing children, her consistency will be challenged. It seems that kids enjoy putting their parents through the "are you really going to follow through this time?" test. It takes a really Big-Girl parent to stay consistent even though her child may be angry with her and the relationship feels strained. In the long run, the relationship will be healthier if the parent acts like a parent and toes the line on obedience. Naughty children who test the limits are not looking for relationship. They are looking for their way. So nothing is lost when the parent is a Big Girl. In fact, ultimately everything is gained.

A Big-Girl mom wrote to me, "My son says I am tough, but he quickly adds, 'she is real.'" That's what being a Big-Girl mom is all about: being strong and real. Children can respect strong if they see that the one meting out the rule is real! Make sure you are "the real deal" so your child will know you aren't playing games. Being "the real deal" means you are consistent in discipline as well as

> **Big-Girl Truth to Live By:**
>
> *Being a Big-Girl mom is all about being strong and real. Children can respect strong if they see that the one meting out the rule is real!*

your own behavior. It should go without saying that you don't ask your child to be obedient in an area where you have no mastery. If you want your child to speak with respect, you must speak with respect. If you want your child to be polite, it behooves you to exemplify politeness. You are the leader in the relationship. Let them know you love them, but you are unwilling to abdicate your authority.

Once children become teenagers, a contract is an effective tool to maintain consistency. If parents and teens can sit down together when things are cool and unruffled and draw up a contract that essentially says, "When you do this, I will do this," and "When I do this, you can expect this," then the family will have an established arbiter for the next stressful event. The boundaries are settled and agreed upon and the consequences are spelled out. That is healthy for the teen as well as the parent.

I have seen Big-Girl moms who keep their copy of the contract close by so that when a disagreement comes up, they can pull it out and say, "Here is what you agreed to, and this is what I agreed to, so this is the way it's going to be, right?"

Big Girls know that they cannot make the relationship with their teenage children a battleground of wills. If they do, they inevitably will be sucked into an emotional maelstrom from which it is very difficult to back out. Establishing rules ahead of time will help you be on top of your own response. It is hard to deal with a mouthy child and not be mouthy yourself if you haven't thought about your discipline approach in advance. Consequently, previous planning for handling situations puts you ahead of the game. Stick to the rules, be kind, and pray.

Not Every Battle Is Worth Fighting

You won't have a contract for everything that happens. You can't because you won't be able to foresee all of the ideas and tricks your very bright children will come up with. You will have to determine what your battlegrounds are. Not every sock on the floor or crumb on the kitchen counter is worthy of a confrontation, unless you are a Little-Girl mom. Then those things can be overwhelming, while some bigger issues are swept aside because they are too difficult to deal with. There are, however, two critical, major battles that cannot and should not be avoided and must be settled early on: (1) respect and (2) trust and truthfulness.

1. **Respect.** Big-Girl moms understand that when respect is eroded, the relationship crumbles and is hard to rebuild. That is why respect needs to be an issue from the time a toddler first attempts to hit you until your adult child moves out of the house. Respect established in early childhood will carry over into adult-

hood. If it has not been rooted early, then it will be a struggle to establish it twenty years down the line.

Big-Girl moms know that it is all right for children to be angry, but they must be angry in a respectful way. Name calling, hitting, spitting, biting, and screaming at a parent, sibling, or friend is not acceptable. Big-Girl moms halt that type of angry response immediately.

A Big-Girl mom whose discipline I really respect calls any outrageous verbal lashing out "a crime of the mouth." She will not allow it. She also insists that "sorry" is not enough. If you have offended enough that you need to apologize, you need to name what the apology is for. This keeps records clean and makes children aware of what they have done and why it won't be good to do it again. Left undisciplined, "verbal crimes" are hard to curtail. Again, if a Big-Girl mom is going to curtail this problem in her children, she has to set the example and curtail it in herself. An adult should *never* demean a child by name calling or screaming. (I assume that hitting, spitting, and biting are not options!) If that type of thing is going on in your home, it is imperative that you get help as soon as possible. If you think you have problems now, you haven't seen what will happen later. A good counselor can intervene and help head off a lifetime of heartache.

I think this is a good time to interject a word about spanking. I do not consider spanking and hitting to be the same. Hitting is a knee-jerk reaction to an irritant. Hitting is smacking, slapping, and punching in response to an undesirable behavior. Spanking, on the other hand, is not a reaction. It is a response to be used for guidance and correction. If your child is not "getting it" via talking and time-outs, it is timely to consider spanking. I believe parents are so frightened of losing their child's approval that they are fearful of applying the very prescription that God instructed in the book of Proverbs:

"He who spares the rod hates his son, but he who loves him is careful to discipline him" (Proverbs 13:24 NIV). I believe the key phrase in that verse is "careful to discipline." We all need discipline in order to be brought into line with God's plan for us. Discipline is the tool used to direct our paths when our tendency is to stray.

To spank correctly is to be careful to discipline. It should be done privately. If you need to leave your groceries in the cart and go home in order to administer the discipline in private, it will be worth the inconvenience. Shaming a child is not the point. Making a memorable point is. I think that the current generation of young parents has an unnatural fear of shaming. If your heart is to lovingly correct and you don't make a public display in front of others (including their peers), there should be no shame. The child may be embarrassed for doing a foolish thing and experiencing consequences, but that is part of the learning process. That is not shaming.

When spanking is necessary, a child needs to be told why he is receiving a spanking. The spanking needs to be applied with swiftness (none of this "wait 'til your daddy gets home" Little-Girl stuff), and then he needs to be comforted by being held close until he is calm. Once it is over, it is over. The event does not need to be dragged out and discussed again in the child's presence. If you want to discuss the situation with your husband later, that's okay, but the child needs to go through the correction only once. If he or she offends again, go through the same process until your beloved child understands the behavior is unacceptable and you will not tolerate it. That is training, and many times training is successful only by repetition. Don't despair; eventually your persistence and consistency will pay off.

2. Trust and Truthfulness. Trust and truthfulness are about character. Big-Girl moms know that every child will lie from time to time. The key to dealing with it is not in being horrified, but in staying alert enough to pick up on the signs that truth is being compromised. I love what my son and daughter-in-law do with their children. (Oh, that I would have been so wise so young!) If in doubt about one of their children's responses, they say, "Truth?" This gives the child a chance to recant, come clean, and avoid the embarrassment of being found out. It is a chance to wipe the slate clean.

This grace is what a Big-Girl mom will provide. Human nature, even childish human nature, doesn't like to be found out, but when it is, it needs to be dealt with. I vividly remember an incident that had a profound character-building effect on me when I was about four years old. I loved glasses and couldn't convince anyone that I needed them. I thought they were so cool. So, one day in day care, I noticed that Barbara Malloy had put her gorgeous little blue glasses in her purse that was hanging on a hook in the hallway. Seeing an opportunity to have glasses for myself, I got them out of her purse and tucked them in the front of my shorts. I pulled my shirt down over my tummy with the glasses protruding ever so slightly and went about my activities.

One fact that makes this incident of note is that my mother was the director of the day care center. When it was time for the moms to pick up the kids, I watched Barbara and her mother looking all over for her glasses. I saw my own mother searching for them as well, but I kept quiet because I really wanted those glasses. So after the unsuccessful hunt, I heard Mother apologize to Barbara's mother. She assured her that she would have everyone look for the glasses in the morning.

That night we went home, my secret tucked in my shorts. When we arrived, we had dinner and my mom and dad sat talking in the living room. Being drowsy, I decided to lie down on the sofa and put my head in mother's lap. She pulled me close to snuggle and then patted me on the tummy. "What is this?" she asked. I said, "Nothing." She pulled up my shirt and there they were, Barbara Malloy's glasses. She and my dad were shocked, and I was mad. I hadn't even had the chance to try those glasses on and wear them in my room, and here I was, found out! Mother, who had found her Big-Girl self already, immediately announced that we would take the glasses back and that I would apologize to Barbara. It was that simple.

We got in the car to drive across town to Barbara's home. Mother dabbed at her eyes from time to time as she talked with me about stealing and truthfulness and how this act of mine impacted Barbara and her mother. Daddy drove and only commented a time or two, but he said enough for me to know that I had transgressed a really big rule of life. I got the seriousness of it! I was made aware that stealing and lying were not acceptable, and there would be grave consequences!

When we arrived at Barbara's house, her mother was sitting on the front steps, and Barbara was playing on the sidewalk. I had to get out of the car and walk up to them with my mortified mother. She explained, gave the glasses back, and then turned to me so I could make my explanations! There would be no shyness or refusal to speak here. I had transgressed a major moral code in our family and I *would* correct it. Case closed.

Barbara and her mother accepted my apology, and then I had to get back in the car and ride across town with my mom and dad. They had made a believer out of me at that tender age. Lying and stealing would not be tolerated at our house. I knew I had embarrassed and humiliated them, but they were more interested in my character than any of that. Mother could have acted as if she just found the glasses the next day and saved us all quite a night, but she knew my character development was more important than her reputation or my dad's discomfort over what I had done.

PRINCIPLES FOR BIG-GIRL MOMS
OF GROWN CHILDREN

Let Go

Being a Big-Girl mom doesn't mean it is easy to let your children go as they grow and mature. Although it is the healthy thing to do, letting go of children just doesn't feel right. After spending almost two decades making sure they are taken care of, you have to let them go, just when it looks as if you might have accomplished a good thing. Also, letting go is a process, not a one-time event.

The process looks something like this: The relationship with our children is like a two-sided scale, the old-fashioned kind that holds weights on one side and objects to be weighed on the other. Well, when it comes to being a mother, we start out as the heavyweight in the relationship. The child is the lightweight. Because of your significance and power and responsibility, your side of the scale is at the bottom; his side is at the top. You determine everything in his life because your side is the weighty side, but as the years pass, you slowly become the lightweight in the relationship and he becomes the heavyweight.

Big-Girl moms know that this is okay; it is the way it should be. They don't kick against it and make it into some awful event. The fact is, this is what you have worked for. This is what you have trained your children for, and when it finally happens, it is a lovely experience. The hard part is realizing that you are losing your status as a heavyweight. It is hard to realize you are not in control. It is difficult to face the fact that you are no longer needed in the same way that you once were. In fact, you are no longer even wanted in the same way. To gracefully accept this truth is a real turning point in the relationship as well as in your sense of yourself. When you become the lightweight, you recognize that you can no longer intervene, interfere, or interject yourself into your child's life. Unless you are invited, it is not appropriate. This is the way it should be! Big-Girl moms understand this.

I once met a wonderful woman who raised five children virtually alone. She told me that on their eighteenth birthdays, she wrapped up a pair of apron strings for each one. This was their rite of passage. They had new responsibilities that included being responsible for themselves. Mama was a Big-Girl mom who wanted her children to be Big Girls and Big Boys. In fact, her gift of the apron strings gave them permission to be just that! This permission frees young adults from having to pull away and tiptoe around Mama so she won't be upset and still feel significant. That is a Little-Girl mom response, and it is a burden to her children.

Big-Girl moms know when to let go and they know how to take care of themselves. They don't put their grown children in a position to be caring for them. This is especially true if Mama is healthy and able to fend for herself. Unless you are ill and have no other means of being cared for, your children should be free to take care of themselves and their families without being burdened with taking care of Mama. That of course does not preclude having an ongoing relationship, but it does eliminate making the children responsible for your happiness.

Give Up Responsibility

Once your child leaves home and you are no longer financially responsible for him, you no longer have authority nor responsibility in his life. That's good news. Big Girls understand this and don't keep taking responsibility for children who don't live at home. I have seen a number of moms who still take care of their children's business. They do their grown son's wash and make sure that he has milk and bread in his fridge. They check up on their grown daughter, making sure she is eating well and not staying out too late. Once a child is paying his own way, he is no longer answerable to his parents.

On the flip side, Big Girls maintain their responsibility as long as they have authority even though it may be hard. They don't bail out when the parenting job is theirs to do! If a child is not paying his own way but lives off his parents, then he is still under their authority, no matter how old he is. Often, when an adult child has not assumed his or her place in society and remains at home, and has been allowed to be the governing force in the home, the roles and boundaries become confused. But if the "under roof, under rule" absolute has been maintained, it is easier to let everyone know, "This is your position." When adult children are able to provide for their basic needs, they need to be out of the house. These days, many grown children don't want to leave, mostly for economic reasons. They would rather have a little money in their pocket than the freedom of their own apartment. This attitude marks a real switch from the previous generation, but for whatever reason, it is still healthier for grown children to have their own roof. It is a rite of passage that no one should fail to make.

Set Boundaries

One of the joys of growing older is getting to know your children as adults. This is a great privilege that has to be handled with care because if you treat your children as you did when they were children, you will find yourself in another struggle. Just as when they were children, good strong boundaries will make the adult relationship workable. Big-Girl moms know and understand this; Little-Girl moms will kick against this and get their feelings hurt.

Here are some of the boundaries that will make a relationship with your adult children work well:

- If you live in the same town, always call before dropping in. Make it clear that you would like for them to do the same. This builds mutual respect.

- Be interested but not nosey about their lives. If they want to tell you about something, they will. Don't allow your feelings to be hurt because they don't tell you or they tell someone else first. They are not under obligation.

- If they ask for your counsel, give it. If they don't ask for it and you feel that you have some wisdom to contribute, say, "If you don't mind me giving you advice, I won't mind if you don't take it." At least you have said what you need to say, and your child can choose to take it or not.

- It is imperative to respect your child's mate. Strive to treat him or her as well or better than your own child. Your courtesy can pay off in the long run.

- If your children are not married, try to refrain from asking them when they plan to marry. Trust me, they will let you know. Until then, they would probably rather not discuss it!

- When you have grandchildren, be a Big-Girl grandmother by following your child's wishes about what your grandchildren eat, drink, play with, and watch. Don't side against your child (the parent) with the grandchildren. Don't cut their hair without permission or change their appearance in any way. Getting ears pierced and painting fingernails requires permission. Big Girls know that they are not the parent, and it is imperative to allow the true parent to remain in control. This may seem as if it is a no-brainer, but sometimes when your grandchild asks you for pierced ears or a real kitty cat to take home, it is hard to remember that you are not the parent. Do what is needed to maintain a good relationship with your child, and don't spare your affirming comments about how well they parent. A kind word from someone who has been there can make all the difference.

- Don't preach. By the time your children are grown, they know the truth about spiritual matters. If they have not already embraced the faith that you taught them, continual preaching is not going to change them now. Love them, pray for them, and be an example of the goodness of God in their lives. That will do far more to turn their hearts toward God than all the preaching you could do.

Being a Big-Girl mom has so many payoffs. Your children will more than likely respect you, but just as importantly, you will respect yourself for being a parent and not a child. No matter what choices your child makes along the way, you can know that you did the best you could and chose to be mature when you had other options. A Big-Girl mom will be a blessing in her children's lives from the time they enter her world until they are very grown. There is nothing like a Big-Girl mother. Her children will rise up and bless her. Of that there is no doubt.

Seven

Freedom for Big-Girl Friends

Living Honestly As a True Friend

WHEN I WAS IN JUNIOR HIGH, I walked the mile home from school with one of my girl chums every day. She would drop me off at my house and then proceed to hers, which was three blocks away. When she got there, she would call me, and we would continue our all-important junior-high conversations. So I was stunned when one day we got to my house and she abruptly announced, "I can't be friends with you anymore." I was shocked! "Why?" I asked before I thought better of it. She quickly told me. "You are too bubbly!" "That's it? I'm too bubbly?" "Yes, you are too bubbly." See you around. That was it. End of friendship.

At that young age, the two of us were literal little girls just beginning to explore the journey of relationships with all its twists and turns. I had to learn that friendships are very special, and simply sharing some things in common with another person does not make you true friends. As I think back over some of the friendships I have had in my life, I can see places where I made huge mistakes just because I didn't know how to be a good friend.

The saving grace was that I learned. That's what sets apart Big Girls and Little Girls. It isn't that the Big Girls don't make mistakes. They surely do, but they don't keep making the same mistakes, getting burned and burning others in friendships. They learn what they need to learn and apply it. Unfortunately, some grown women are still Little Girls when it comes to their friendships; they've never learned the value of a strong bond between women.

Friendship is far more sacred than something that can be tossed on a whim: "I like you today but I am through with you tomorrow." Friendship is such a special relationship, in fact, that Jesus said to his disciples, "No longer do I call you slaves, for the slave does not know what his master is doing; but I have called you friends, for all things that I have heard from My Father I have made known to you" (John 15:15). Jesus placed a high value on real friendship, and so should we.

Friendship is a wonderful, voluntary relationship. The wonder of it is that there are no laws to keep friends together, no vows that are spoken before God and man, and no contracts to sign. Big Girls make great friends. Time and distance may come between you, but if you are truly Big-Girl friends, the following blessings of your friendship will only become richer.

BIG-GIRL FRIENDS SAY WHAT THEY MEAN AND MEAN WHAT THEY SAY

You can count on a Big-Girl friend. She doesn't waffle back and forth between feelings and facts. If she says it, you should be able to count on it. You will never have to wonder if she has an ulterior motive. You don't have to guess whether she is upset with you or if she didn't like what you said the last time you were together.

Big-Girl friends understand that the words that pass between them are critical. Part of being a Big Girl is using words—and not pointed body language, innuendos, and sarcasm—to communicate. Using healthy words that "speak" is something that Big Girls are good at. They take the admonition in Ephesians 4 seriously:

> Let no foul or polluting language, nor evil word nor unwholesome or worthless talk [ever] come out of your mouth, but only such [speech] as is good and beneficial to the spiritual progress of others, as is fitting to the need and the occasion, that it may be a blessing and give grace (God's favor) to those who hear it. And do not grieve the Holy Spirit of God [do not offend or vex or sadden Him], by Whom you were sealed (marked, branded as God's own, secured) for the day of redemption (of final deliverance through Christ from evil and the consequences of sin). Let all bitterness and indignation and wrath (passion, rage, bad temper) and resentment (anger, animosity) and quarreling (brawling, clamor, contention) and slander (evil-speaking, abusive or blasphemous language) be banished from you, with all malice (spite, ill will, or baseness of any kind). And become useful and helpful and kind to one another, tenderhearted (compassionate, understanding, loving-hearted), forgiving one another [readily and freely], as God in Christ forgave you. (Ephesians 4:29–32 AMP)

Big Girls respect one another too much to let grouchy, mindless words be spoken. You will never hear a Big Girl saying, "I'm sorry if I hurt your feelings, but I just had to get that off of my chest." Those are the words of a Little Girl who has allowed herself to become frustrated and antsy.

Big-Girl friends know how to go to one another with love and kindness if a problem arises between them. They use wholesome words to say what needs to be said. "The right word at the right time is like a custom-made piece of jewelry, and a wise friend's timely reprimand is like a gold ring slipped on your finger" (Proverbs 25:11–12 MSG).

Jen and Barb are great friends and roommates. Jen is the gregarious "we share all things in common" kind of woman. Barb, on the other hand, is a strong believer that good boundaries make good relationships. They know and understand each other, but once, the refrigerator became an issue between them. Barb often bought specialty items to have on hand for entertaining friends who would drop in to visit. Jen, gregarious soul that she is, felt free to indulge in

> **Big-Girl Truth to Live By:**
>
> *Life is too short to keep nursing a problem between really good friends.*

anything that was in the refrigerator. After replacing the Brie cheese and fruit a couple of times, Barb became annoyed. She loved Jen too much to make a huge issue, but she knew that good boundaries keep good friendships healthy. So she broached the subject one Saturday morning with Jen. She said, "Jen, I love sharing this house with you. You are so fun and so thoughtful, but I need to tell you the disappearing Brie and fruit make me a little anxious. You know it's not the money, but when I expect to go to the fridge and find nice things I can serve our friends, I am taken aback when it's not there. I know you don't mean a thing by it. You would give away the shirt on your back or your last bottle of Perrier, but this is a matter of boundaries. If you would ask if I need whatever I have in the fridge before you nibble on it, I would be so grateful." Jen listened with wide-eyed amazement. It had never occurred to her that nibbling on the cheese was a problem for Barb, but she loved her friend enough to say, "I am so sorry. Of course I'll ask you. I just wasn't thinking. Will you forgive me?" Barb assured Jen that all was forgiven and that they would go on with no hard feelings.

If either of these women were Little Girls, the cheese and fruit would have become a festering sore between them. But because they valued clear communication and respected one another, the issue was dealt with, and they were the better for it.

If a Big Girl needs to say something, she will say it, but it will be expressed with dignity, kindness, and respect. She will say exactly what she means. She will mean what she says. What great security that gives to a relationship. Having a Big-Girl friend means you don't have to wonder where you stand. You always will know.

A Big-Girl friend doesn't hang on to a problem by rehearsing it over and over in her head. Life is too short to keep nursing a problem between really good friends. Of course, it takes two Big Girls to get past it. So often, Little Girls want to keep milking the situation as if the longer they hang on to it, the better they will feel. Big Girls deal with it and let it go! Once it is dealt with, Big Girls are ready to move on.

BIG-GIRL FRIENDS ARE TRUSTWORTHY

There is nothing worse than having to watch your back or wondering whether you can trust someone you call "friend." "Friend" and "trustworthy" should go hand in hand. If you want to be a Big-Girl friend, then you have to choose to protect your friend's privacy and dignity for always. Sometimes that means keeping your mouth shut about something you know about your friend, even if you think it is harmless. You might find yourself in a group where others seem to know all about the issue, but out of respect for your friend, you keep quiet. Your friend's business is not everyone else's business. Even if people think they know something, you don't have to add to their conversation. That's called being trustworthy.

My friend Carolyn is that kind of friend. She can keep a confidence. I have seen her faithfully handle private information not only for me but for others for over thirty years. She can be trusted. If we ever share anything that is okay for us to discuss and is confidential we often say, "Now this is 'grave' talk." What we mean is that we will take the conversation to our grave. A Big Girl knows how to handle a friend's "grave talk," because she is trustworthy.

BIG-GIRL FRIENDS GUARD EACH OTHER WITH TRUTH

Friends don't let friends do foolish things without speaking up. That's one of the good things about being a friend. It gives you the right to express concern, and if your friend is truly a Big Girl, she will want to hear you. One of my Big-Girl friends was on the threshold of making a gigantic mistake by marrying a man who was diametrically opposed to everything she stood for. It was as if she were under a spell. Through some personal interactions with me, he showed his true colors. There was no way I could be silent. I had to say to my friend, "What are you thinking?" Even if she didn't want to hear it, I had to say it. She was too precious a person to just let her wander off into the sad life for which she was headed.

Big-Girl friends can be trusted to call you into accountability if you stray too far off the path. And, of course, they will love you anyway. My friend who was getting ready to plunge into the marital abyss came to her senses, was affirmed by other trusted friends, and called off the wedding. It didn't take her long to see that she had been on the verge of a devastating situation. Today she is married to the love of her life. She cannot believe she ever considered the other man.

This anonymous quotation sums up the trust Big-Girl friends share: "A woman once commented, 'The best thing a friend ever told me while I was in depression was, "You know we're getting pretty tired of this. When are you going to do something about it?" That's all it took. I went for help right away.'" Big Girls don't gang up

> ## Big-Girl Truth to Live By:
>
> *When you love a friend and she knows it, you can be her best encourager to do what is right and good.*

on one another, but when you know that a person you love is making choices that will harm her and is living at a level lower than she has to, you speak up. When a friend loves you and you know it, she can be your best encourager to do what is right and good. Sometimes girlfriends can do that when relatives fail. Often, they have too much baggage and are too close to the situation. A friend, on the other hand, is a relationship of choice. If the friendship is healthy and in good repair, who better to say what you need to hear than your friend?

BIG GIRLS SHARE THEIR FRIENDS WITH FRIENDS

One of the most fun things in life is meeting the friends of friends and finding out how much you have in common. Big Girls don't play the possessive game. They don't try to keep their friends to themselves. Instead they are thrilled when new circles of friends come together and expand.

I have just met Ellie, the friend of a friend. I liked her the minute I met her and enjoyed conversation with her immediately. I want to know more about Ellie. I want to spend more time with her and will no doubt have that opportunity. But my interest in her will never diminish my friendship with the woman who introduced us. It can only make all of our relationships richer.

Jealousy is an obvious enemy that quickly darkens the brightness of a friendship. So when Big Girls share their friends, they do so with an open hand. They don't try to hang on with a death grip to the special people in their life. They know that unless there is freedom in a relationship, the relationship is not authentic. Big Girls aren't threatened by a new friend of a friend. They just widen their circle and take her in. There is always enough love for another friend.

BIG-GIRL FRIENDS CAN COME AND GO WITHOUT PRESSURE

There is nothing worse than feeling pressure from a friend, especially if it is the kind of pressure that suggests you're not doing enough. Big-Girl friends give one another a lot of space. There is room to come and go without feeling as if you are falling short in some way. Friendship means freedom. To feel pressure is to dampen that freedom. If you are friends with someone who counts calls and keeps score on visits, you are connected to a Little Girl who needs to grow up in her relational understanding.

One of the most mature relationships I have is with my friend Betsy, who moved away from my town. We rarely talk on the phone. We don't have to. We just have a *knowing* that we are a phone call away. If either of us had a need or a want, the other would drop whatever she was doing and make herself available to meet it. Other than that, we don't need a lot of assurances between us. There is no fear that the relationship will become less valuable or that our caring for each other will be less over time. We are friends. That was settled years ago, and that's just the way it is. I feel no pressure from her, and she feels none from me. That's the way we like it.

BIG GIRLS DON'T DEMAND CONFORMITY IN THEIR FRIENDS

Differences make for interesting friends. Big Girls can handle the differences and not feel threatened by their friends' diversity. If your friends were all just like you, life would be so boring! Big Girls don't have to have friends who talk and dress just like they do in order to feel comfortable. They love their friends for what they both can bring to the table without compromising one another's integrity.

One of my good friends is a real athlete, I mean the kind who takes her athletic endeavors seriously. When we were both younger, we played racquetball together. She had a deadly smash ball that left me searching and swinging at the air every time we played. She was a class-A competitor. I have never been known for my athletic prowess, but we managed to be friends in spite of this difference. I think she played racquetball with me just to be nice— in fact I know she did—but we had fun and laughed together. She didn't get frustrated with me, and I wasn't intimidated by her. We were friends first and foremost. The differences in our abilities and our interests were secondary.

Some of my Big-Girl friends are from a different ethnic

background than I am. They are African-American. I am Anglo-Saxon. We look different, our backgrounds are different, our cultures are different, and when we talk, we quickly realize that our views of life are quite different. If we allow our differences to be the major emphasis in our friendships, we never would be friends. Of course, if we failed to acknowledge the differences, we would be fooling ourselves. Again, Big Girls know how to talk about differences without being threatened or becoming defensive. Some of the sweetest, most honest discussions I have had have taken place around dinner tables with some of my black sisters. We unburden ourselves freely. They speak from their experience and I from mine. When all is said and done, we can know that we have a deeper understanding of one another and are that much closer together.

Differences make for interesting friends and allow you to learn from each other if condemnation is not a part of the relationship.

I'll never forget the time one of my friends—a beautiful, intelligent accomplished woman of color—told me that she had had a stalker. I was horrified. I asked, "Has he been caught?" She said, "No. I haven't reported him because I just cannot bear to see another black man put in jail." I was amazed. I could not respond to the situation that way through my eyes, but she gave me a glimpse of it through her eyes. She allowed me to "see through her glasses" for just a moment, and I realized, if ever so slightly, how her life experience had formed her thinking. I could not argue with her, nor should I have, because she was giving me an understanding of herself.

We all come to our relationships with very different experiences. Big Girls can give credence to their friends' experiences without having lived them themselves. Whatever your life experience is, if you haven't walked in your friends' shoes, you can't totally know what they feel. Big Girls understand that truth and make room for the differences. Big Girls let others feel what they feel without judgment. They celebrate differences and learn from one another without condemnation. Opening yourself to this kind of relationship is a Big-Girl choice, because sometimes another person's experience and interpretation of that experience can run completely counter to what you believe to be true. That is why dialog is good and necessary. Big Girls can handle it. They know that not everyone has to think alike. People have to be allowed to be who they are.

A spirit of condemnation can easily rise up within a Little Girl who is threatened by others' differences. Condemnation is the pronouncement of an accusation and a sentence: "You are this; therefore, this is what I will do about it." However, when a friend watches another friend's behavior slip off the mark, sound judgment compels her to say, "I see the problem, and I will not sugarcoat it. But I will examine my own heart and get the junk out of it before I would dare to reach over and try to scrape the junk out of your heart." I love this passage from *The Message* that addresses how we are to deal with one another:

> Don't pick on people, jump on their failures, criticize their faults—unless, of course, you want the same treatment. That critical spirit has a way of boomeranging. It's easy to see a smudge on your neighbor's face and be oblivious to the ugly sneer on your own. Do you have the nerve to say, "Let me wash your face for you," when your own face is distorted by contempt? It's this whole traveling road-show mentality all over again, playing a holier-than-thou part instead of just living your part. Wipe that ugly sneer off your own face, and you might be fit to offer a washcloth to your neighbor. (Matthew 7:1–5)

A friend of mine told of this situation in her own life when we were discussing Big-Girl friendships: "One of my best friends—we've known each other since seventh grade—is a non-Christian woman who's been in a lesbian relationship for more than ten years. I think I nearly destroyed our friendship when she first told me about her transition to a gay lifestyle, and as a good Christian I thought it my duty to scold her. But fortunately she was gracious and indulged my judgmental approach, and I realized quickly that it's far more important (and biblical, since she's not a Christian yet) just to love her. No matter what choices she makes, I think we have a pretty special, and hopefully lifelong, friendship."

Little Girls get skittish and run. It takes really Big Girls to accept differences and still love one another unconditionally.

Big-Girl Friends Don't Bail When Trouble Comes

You can count on a Big-Girl friend to be there for you when trouble comes, even if it is really sticky trouble that most people would not want to be involved in. Big-Girl friends stand by you through the stuff of life even if it is inconvenient, ill timed, or difficult. "The highest privilege there is, is the privilege of being allowed to share another's pain. You talk about your pleasures to your acquaintances; you talk about your troubles to your friends."[1]

I am an only child, so some of the difficulties I have faced have been rather lonely vigils. When my father was ill and dying, I had a couple of friends who stood by all the way through. One was my friend Susie. She helped me do things that usually only sisters would do, like moving my parents from one place to another. She was at my parents' home the morning after my father died. She brought a couple more Big-Girl friends with her. They tackled the sad business of cleaning up the room where he had been bedridden.

When our family returned to the house, it was clean and in order. All the hospital equipment was gone. Susie came along and did the tough stuff. She was always cheerful. She never complained, and if there was a tough job to tackle, she was first to volunteer. Susie is a Big-Girl friend who is always reliable when trouble comes.

Lynda is my Big-Girl friend who is steadfast in encouragement and prayer. She lives in another state. We met at a conference several years ago, and I immediately recognized her as a Big Girl. She had a life and wasn't looking for another friend to add to her healthy collection. I had a life too, and seeking out another friend wasn't on my agenda, but we just hit it off in spite of our mutual lack of interest in adding any relationships to our lives.

As we chatted, we recognized we had much in common. God knit our hearts together, and although we have been in the same place only half a dozen times in the past three or four years, we have one of those "I'll be there for you" friendships. If I want to do some serious praying, Lynda is one of the first people I call. She also is a wonderful sounding board and is available to work through some perplexing issues. She takes the time for me when she doesn't have the time. That's a friend.

Big Girls are there for their friends in whatever capacity they are needed. If there is trouble, they will support, comfort, pray, and do what needs to be done. If you are in trouble, your Big-Girl friends won't make your situation about themselves and all that they are doing. You can count on that. They will come and go leaving health and kindness behind them.

BIG-GIRL FRIENDS ARE NOT AFRAID OF ONE ANOTHER

Big Girls don't operate on a fear basis with anyone. They have learned that victims are motivated by fear. Big Girls won't give in to being victims. If they are afraid, they turn toward the Word of God and their faith. They don't back down and close the shutters on their heart because they fear that someone will disapprove or be angry. This is especially true in their friendships. Healthy relationships are never based on fear. Big-Girl friendships are free of the fear of rejection, abandonment, and criticism.

This familiar quote by William Penn says it so well:

> Oh the comfort, the inexpressible comfort of feeling safe with a person; having neither to weigh thoughts nor measure words, but to pour them all out, just as they are, chaff and grain together, knowing that a faithful hand will take and sift them, keeping what is worth keeping, and then, with the breath of kindness, blow the rest away.[2]

As I've mentioned earlier, if Big Girls have hard issues to discuss between them, they do it with kindness and gentleness. They never resort to the use of fear or intimidation. You don't have to hide who you really are from a true Big-Girl friend. You can be yourself—the good, the bad, and the ugly—in front of your Big-Girl friend, and she will never change her opinion of you.

I know a woman whose first response to most things that she hears is, "No, I don't think so." Needless to say, she doesn't have a lot of people around her who feel really comfortable discussing what they think. I know that I can't change people whose ideas differ from mine, but I can choose how I respond to them. I can listen without offering a comment. I can allow a friend to process her thoughts with me without having to interject my "yes, but" into the conversation. I can wait until I am asked before I offer an opinion. These are the ways I have learned to be a Big-Girl friend who is approachable. Big Girls are comfortable with just listening.

They know they can't fix the world, but they can offer a listening ear and a heart of compassion to their friends.

BIG-GIRL FRIENDS DEPEND FIRST ON GOD, THEN ON EACH OTHER

Big Girls know that the Light at the end of every tunnel is God. He is the Alpha and the Omega, the Beginning and the End. He is the source of all hope and the anchor in every storm. So Big Girls know their dependence has to be on Him. Their relationship with Him is the premier relationship in their lives, and they build on it every day.

God is the only Friend who is always there, who always has your best interests in His heart, who is always behind the scenes working everything together for good. He knows the whole story of your life because He is the Author of your biography. He knows the last chapter, and He thinks you are wonderful. He is the All in All and must be your All in All. Apart from Him, you can do nothing. Knowing these things, Big Girls depend on God first. They cling to His promise: "Call to Me and I will answer you and show you great and mighty things, fenced in and hidden, which you do not know (do not distinguish and recognize, have knowledge of and understand)" (Jeremiah 33:3 AMP).

After Big Girls call to the Lord and know that He is with them and totally sovereign over every situation, they call their Big-Girl friends if they want a human touch, someone to come alongside them in a human way. That is the blessing of friendship. God is our Shepherd, but we can find comfort sometimes in rubbing shoulders with other wooly sheep that are just as much in need of a Shepherd as we are. Big-Girl friends know they can't fix every hurt or soothe every pain. They know that prayer is the best thing they can do for a friend; holding her hand is second. Big-Girl friends just know.

One of the greatest joys in life is friendship. I love this quote from our country's colonial times: "A true friend unbosoms freely, advises justly, assists readily, adventures boldly, takes all patiently, defends courageously, and continues a friend unchangeably."[3]

The most important aspect of friendship is doing what is best for your friend even when it hurts you. This anonymous poem has sharpened my heart when I think of my friends.

> My friend, beware of me, lest I should do
> the very thing I'd sooner die than do—
> In some way crucify the Christ in you.
> If you are called to some great sacrifice,
> and I should come to you with frightened eyes
> and cry, "Take care, take care, be wise, be wise!"
> See through my softness then, a friend's attack,
> and bid me get me straight behind your back,
> to your own conscience to your God be true,
> lest I play Satan to the Christ in you!
> And I would humbly ask of you in turn
> that if someday in me love's fires should burn
> to whiteness, and a voice should call
> bidding me leave my little for God's all—
> If need be, you would thrust me from your side
> So keep love loyal to the crucified!

Eight

Courage for Big Girls Facing Conflict

Navigating the Pain and Finding Resolution

ONFLICT IS LIKE THE FLU. No one wants to go through it, but everyone needs to be prepared just in case!

Big Girls know that conflict is part of life. It isn't something to go looking for. It isn't enjoyable. But when it comes, a Big Girl is prepared to handle it with wisdom and grace.

Walking through conflict isn't something you can just *choose* to do well. You have *to learn* to do it well. The Big Girl's first lessons in conflict usually start in the home. Conflict is part of family life from time to time, and how it is resolved in your home has a lot of influence on how your conflict-resolution skills are developed. I have a friend who looks back on her wedding-day experience grinning and grimacing at the same time. It was one of those affairs you just want to shake your head at and say, "Yikes, families!" She told me, "At my wedding, my mom's stepmother insisted upon wearing a dress that was almost identical to my mother's, despite the fact that my grandfather and one of my aunts encouraged her to respect my mom and pick something else to wear (she had options). She refused and I was livid, but in my great wisdom I pouted and whined to others rather than confronting her about it. Wasn't that brilliant? Everyone knew how mad I was, and they couldn't do anything about it—they'd already tried! Not only did my little fit fail to accomplish anything but put a damper on my wedding, my frustration made other people anxious too!" Ever been there? How much fun is one of those events? I think almost all of us have a "family feud" story we could tell.

Unless you came from a home where conflict was handled with extraordinary wisdom and grace and where true resolution was usually achieved, you probably don't have the skills you need to resolve conflict peaceably. If you find conflict extremely hard to face, or if you find yourself in conflict more times than you would like to mention, it could be that your skills are faulty. That's the bad news. The good news is that you are not alone, nor is your deficit permanent. You can keep growing and learning.

How *Not* to Handle Conflict

People attempt to solve conflicts in several ways that are common but ineffective. See if you recognize any of these not-so-helpful Little-Girl patterns in your conflict-resolution styles.

• *Ignoring conflict, hoping it will go away.* It is true that by ignoring the problem, there may be a truce for a while. Eventually, however, the old conflict issue will erupt, and you will be faced with having to go through the same old stuff one more time. If you are married, you know that if you don't handle conflicts with skill, you will face them over and over. Ignoring conflicts does allow a temporary scab to form, but it is easily dislodged, allowing the pain and bleeding to start all over again. Ignoring conflict only guarantees that it will rear its same ugly head again and again.

- *Pouting about it, hoping someone will notice.* When someone pouts, she might as well scream. She brings a palpable tension into the room and forces others to tiptoe around the problem. Pouting is ignoring with a lot of power. It is hostage taking. It is the manifestation of the unspoken message, "I choose not to talk about this." Everyone in the situation is left to wonder when things will be normal. "Will we ever talk about it?" They learn to change their normal way of behaving until the pouter decides to quit holding everyone hostage. Big Girls and Boys will eventually figure out that they don't have to be held hostage by a pouter and will refuse to change their normal way of behaving, diffusing the pouter's power. They will learn to ignore her, like they ignore the one who cries wolf. They will refuse to stick around and listen to the silent screaming and will leave the pouter alone with her anger until she's ready to engage. Pouting doesn't work.

- *Fussing about unrelated issues.* Often conflict, in the form of bickering and fussing, swirls perpetually around a great deal of little things—things like forgetting to turn off lights or take out the garbage, parking the car too close to the garage wall, not calling often enough, or even burning the toast. It can be anything. Dissension that is ongoing and nonspecific like this usually indicates a singular underlying issue, such as feeling unappreciated, neglected, ignored, or taken advantage of. Sometimes the conflict might be the result of a one-time incident that has been left to fester. Whatever the cause, there will be no peace until it is resolved. Sometimes, it takes a third party to get to the root of the situation. Just letting things go and go until they erupt one more time is never wise. Big Girls know there is something under the surface that is causing the trouble and are willing to look for it in order to deal with it.

- *Exploding in anger.* Explosive responses to assumed hurts usually come in the form of angry outbursts that cause everyone to walk on eggshells. Anger works because when it is delivered with a barrage of words and pointed body language, it commands everyone's attention. Anger works because it works! People who are within earshot usually become submissive if the outburst is loud or long enough. Gaining someone's submission, however, does not resolve the conflict. That is just more hostage-taking behavior. That is giving in to rage. Big Girls don't need rage; they use words that are

> **Big-Girl Truth to Live By:**
>
> *Ignoring conflict only guarantees that it will rear its same ugly head again and again.*

clear and precise. If they want someone's attention, they simply seize the moment and say, "I want to talk with you. I would like to set up a time to talk that is convenient and will allow us some ability to focus. This is extremely important to me and there is a lot on the line here." When angry responses flow back and forth, it's good to have a let's-cool-down-and-talk-in-adult-terms meeting. Most people don't want to cause angry people to become more volatile, but angry people need to have a place where they will know they can be heard. If you want to be a conflict solver, you can offer that place and then keep your angry person focused on using it. If you are the angry person, then insist on a place of meeting. Make it clear that the issue is important to you and that there is a lot at stake. Meet with some solution in mind.

None of the above conflict-resolution styles—ignoring, pouting, fussing, or exploding—is effective in resolving anything. While it may appear that you are making peace by ignoring it or turning inward with it, the truth is, nothing is resolved. Conflict resolution has to be actively pursued with the emphasis on *resolu-*

tion and a de-emphasis on *conflict*. That's the goal for a Big Girl. She wants to see the best come out of the situation.

Consider the story of this woman who went looking for resolution to a serious conflict with her housemate:

"This woman and I live in the same house. While we were living together, I had a baby. Three days after I gave birth, this woman also had a baby. We were alone—there wasn't anyone else in the house except for the two of us. The infant son of this woman died one night when she rolled over on him in her sleep. She got up in the middle of the night and took my son—I was sound asleep, mind you!—and put him at her breast and put her dead son at my breast. When I got up in the morning to nurse my son, here was this dead baby! But when I looked at him in the morning light, I saw immediately that he wasn't my baby."

"Not so!" said the other woman. "The living one's mine; the dead one's yours."

The first woman countered, "No! Your son's the dead one; mine's the living one."

They went back and forth this way in front of the king.

The king said, "What are we to do? This woman says, 'The living son is mine and the dead one is yours,' and this woman says, 'No, the dead one's yours and the living one's mine.'"

After a moment the king said, "Bring me a sword." They brought the sword to the king.

Then he said, "Cut the living baby in two—give half to one and half to the other."

The real mother of the living baby was overcome with emotion for her son and said, "Oh no, master! Give her the whole baby alive; don't kill him!"

But the other one said, "If I can't have him, you can't have him—cut away!"

The king gave his decision: "Give the living baby to the first woman. Nobody is going to kill this baby. She is the real mother." (1 Kings 3:17–27 MSG)

Big Girls, such as this real mother, are not interested in punishment or retribution, no matter how desperate their situation. They have a heart for resolution. They want the air cleared, the people involved released from the tension and strain of the situation, and a new way of looking at things brought to the forefront. This attitude toward conflict is a choice, just like so many things in life. When we are hurt, it is so easy to go to our "favorite bad feeling" (that feeling that comforts us). For most of us, that bad feeling does not include wanting what might be best. We might be like the bitter woman who was so angry that she preferred the baby die rather than live. But the real mother, the Big-Girl mother, was willing to sacrifice justice for her son. Most of us just want justice, especially if it is for the other person! But Big Girls know that God is a God of reconciliation. He never desires to leave things in turmoil while His girls sit in the middle of it.

THE PRIME RULE OF CONFLICT RESOLUTION: PURSUE PEACE

I love Romans 12:18, which says, "If it is possible, as far as it depends on you, live at peace with everyone" (NIV). Big Girls make every effort to live at peace with others and to bring resolution to divided situations. Pursuing peace is an active process. It does not mean looking for peace at any price or ignoring the problem. That is a recipe for ongoing conflict without resolution. Big Girls understand that it takes two to resolve any conflict.

There are those who assume that if they just do the right thing, then everything will turn out favorably. That is really wishful thinking. True resolution requires two people who desire the same result: peace. If only one desires it, then it will never be achieved. Things can get better, and ways of relating can be rearranged, but there will never be peace between the two parties.

A Big Girl knows that she can't make someone else want peace with her. God knows that, too, so the good news is that you are not responsible to bring peace to a situation where there is no cooperation. You are responsible to be at peace only as much as you can be on your own. A friend who told me about one of these situations in her life makes the point well.

> I was once promoted to a supervisory position during a time when my colleagues and I were involved in a department-wide salary dispute. After action was taken and salaries were adjusted, one employee remained dissatisfied. She began to shirk responsibilities and drag down coworkers' morale with her constant complaints. Although I had socialized with her outside the office and considered her a friend, I eventually had to take disciplinary action—on the advice of *my* supervisors—when she wouldn't temper her behavior and do her job. Our friendship was essentially severed when my firm approach triggered her anger and she quit without giving notice. We've never spoken since, and that saddens me, but I'm at peace about my attempts to resolve the issue before it came to that.

Not everything that is broken can be fixed. Big Girls know that and are willing to leave some situations unresolved when they have done all they can.

Here are some Big-Girl ways to seek peace.

HEAD OFF CONFLICT BEFORE IT STARTS

In many cases you can avoid conflict by overlooking others' transgressions toward you. Try to do this whenever possible. The Scriptures say, "A man's discretion makes him slow to anger, and it is his glory to overlook a transgression" (Proverbs 19:11). If you can avoid the conflict in the first place, then you won't have to deal with trying to resolve the problem. I am convinced most of the issues that tie us in knots are not worth the effort. You can overlook a transgression, but not a conflict. If a conflict does occur, it has to be resolved or at least the attempt must be made.

Sometimes it helps to sleep on something before you get into it. I am always amazed at how different things look in the morning. If it is an issue that needs to be handled, it will still be an issue in the morning. The problem may not change, but a good night's sleep will often give clarity to your perspective.

ASK GOD FOR WISDOM

The Lord promises in James 1:5–8:

> If any of you lacks wisdom, let him ask of God, who gives to all liberally and without reproach, and it will be given to him. But let him ask in faith, with no doubting, for he who doubts is like a wave of the sea driven and tossed by the wind. For let not that man suppose that he will receive anything from the Lord; he is a double-minded man, unstable in all his ways. (NKJV)

Big Girls know that the only wisdom we have comes from God. He invites us to ask Him what to do when we don't know what to do. He will answer, but He is insistent that we believe Him when the wisdom comes. He wants us to take Him at His word without doubting and saying, "Well, I'm not sure about that." That kind of double-mindedness will get you nowhere. Big Girls are single-minded. When they ask God for help and He tells them what to do in their minds, they compare it to His Word, and if it lines up, they go with it.

SEEK TO UNDERSTAND RATHER THAN TO BE UNDERSTOOD

It is so important to be cool headed enough to stop and remember that in any conflict, there are at least two sides. You may have a side that you believe is absolutely bulletproof. You may know you are right. You may know the other person is wrong, but if you are going to pursue peace as much as it is within you, it is critical that you listen to the argument your opponent puts forth. Stopping up your ears to anything that might come from an opposing side is immaturity. If you listen, you may hear the clue you need to bring resolution. Big Girls really value listening. Little Girls lean more toward doing a lot of talking.

SPEAK THE TRUTH IN LOVE

Truth is the *reality* that lies clearly before you. It is not your assumption or your hope. It is the real thing that you see in front of you. Truth spoken with love doesn't necessarily express what the other person *wants* to hear but what the other person *needs* to hear. "But speaking the truth in love, we are to grow up in all aspects into Him, who is the head, even Christ" (Ephesians 4:15). It takes a Big Girl to do this, because sometimes in trying to resolve a conflict it is tempting to say what the other person wants to hear just so everything can be smoothed over.

To get to the root of a problem and to establish a truly peaceful result, the truth has to be spoken. A word of caution here: You have to be sure you know the truth of the matter before you speak. A good way to approach a situation is to say, "Please correct me if you believe that I am wrong, but I understand that you said/did/meant _____."

This gives the person an open door to refute the "truth" that you believe you know, but it also lets that person know that you know.

When I was much younger, I was in a situation where I needed

Big-Girl Truth to Live By:

When you ask God for wisdom, He will give it. But He will insist that you believe Him rather than waver in doubt.

some help understanding what on earth was going on in a certain relationship that was fraught with anxiety, anger, and misunderstanding.

I was trying to salvage a relationship that was based on some faulty beliefs. The more I tried to fix it, the more problematic it became. I blamed the other person, blamed the situation, blamed other people who were part of the equation, and was generally miserable.

I encountered a wise counselor who dared to speak truth to me. She was more concerned for the big-picture outcome of my life than she was for the nitty gritty details that were consuming my attention. She took the time and expended the energy to say, "I understand your situation, but here is where you are missing it and contributing to the problem." She looked beyond my protests and instinct for self-protection and said, "The problem is you and the way that you think." I didn't want to hear that. I wanted to be totally exonerated from having a part in the chaos and confusion of the relationship.

But she loved me enough to tell me the truth, even though I really didn't want to hear it. Only in hearing and acknowledging the truth about myself could I grab hold of my thinking and correct my faulty perceptions. Ultimately, because of that situation, I was able to see and to live the truth more and more. Since we have the good word that "truth will set you free," I have loved the truth and made every effort to live in it ever since. Big Girls love the truth!

Always leave room for mercy. Don't assume that because you know another person's heart you automatically know the truth. In his book *When Bad Christians Happen to Good People,* Dave Burchett writes, "I remember the time I criticized a Christian friend about his angry explosion over what seemed to be a trivial issue. I made some judgmental remarks about his faith. Then I found out that his mother had died the day before. I felt like a world-class weasel. . . . ."[1] Don't assume that you know another's motives. If you are speaking the truth, make sure it is truth.

ASK YOURSELF, "WHAT PART DO I PLAY IN THE PROBLEM?"

If there is a conflict then you have a role in it. Your role may be a passive one, in which you do not do what you ought to do. Or your contribution may be an unrealistic expectation. You may be looking for a behavior that just isn't going to happen, and therefore you are disappointed, and this causes conflict. Or perhaps you are refusing to look at how you have enabled behavior that has brought you to the conflict. Although your opponent may be wrong, maybe he or she has chosen that path because you have allowed it. Maybe you have ignored the problem, hoping it would go away, acting as if everything is all right when you knew it really wasn't.

Stacy knew that her fifteen-year-old son, Chad, smoked pot. She had found a couple of joints in his room. She confronted him on it a time or two, but he denied it and so she just left it alone. "At least he isn't doing the hard stuff," she reasoned. Chad knew that she knew but wasn't going to do anything about it. Stacy stayed fearful and self-doubting. What had she done that caused her son to smoke weed? What else was he doing? She couldn't bear to know. She was really broken hearted the night the police called to tell her they were holding Chad at the police station for selling drugs. When she hung up the phone, all she could mouth was, "Why, why, why?"

Big Girls are able to take an honest look at their role and their actions in conflict. It is a sign of maturity to be able to say to yourself, "I have contributed to the conflict by ignoring the problem, denying the issue, telling myself there was nothing I could do, fearing the anger of the other person, living like a victim. It takes courage to take this kind of hard look at ourselves and then see what we can do.

One of the best ways I know to do that is to simply ask God to show you yourself. "Search me, O God, and know my heart; try me and know my anxious thoughts; and see if there be any hurtful way in me and lead me in the everlasting way" (Psalm 139:23–24). God is faithful to answer the cry of a sincere heart.

CREATE A CRISIS AS A PATH TO PEACE

When something has been swept under the rug for a long time and there has been no resolution of the underlying issues that cause conflict, Big Girls sometimes have to create a crisis. Creating a crisis is like setting a controlled burn in the forest. These fires are set to burn off the undergrowth in order to prevent a huge conflagration later. The goal of creating the crisis is to bring peace in the long run.

I have a good friend whom I'll call Darla. Darla came from a home where struggles and misunderstandings were always shoved under the carpet. No one ever spoke of the unhappiness, but everyone was unhappy. Words of affirmation were seldom if ever heard, but cutting remarks and criticisms were frequent.

Darla grew up and then dealt with the pain she carried from her upbringing. She had detached herself from her family of origin by moving several states away. That was how she maintained a peace with them, but she knew it was tenuous at best.

When she discovered that her mother and father had turned their caustic, critical words on their grandson, Darla's nephew, she could stand it no more.

Darla had become a Big Girl who understood she couldn't keep running from ongoing struggles. She made plane reservations and flew back to her hometown. She went home and sat down with her parents to bring the issues to the surface. She asked them to tell her what was at the root of the critical comments directed toward her and now toward their grandson, Jim.

The room fell silent.

They could not believe that Darla had brought up the issue, but the crisis had been created. It no longer could be avoided.

Darla's parents began to list reasons why they were critical of her. She listened. If she was guilty, she asked their forgiveness. If she wasn't guilty, she said, "I'm sorry you feel that way." Once they had emptied their arsenal, she asked if there was anything else they had to say. She waited. They finally said, "No," and then Darla made a Big-Girl statement: "Then I assume we are clear. From now on, critical, sarcastic comments will not be part of our relationship. If you call me or I call you and the criticism begins, I will have to hang up. We will talk another day." When Darla left, her parents were a little cool, but the crisis she had created marked a new day in their relationship.

When they spoke to each other, the conversations were upbeat. If Darla's parents became critical and sarcastic, she graciously concluded the conversation and waited to talk another day. It only took about three calls like that for everything to completely change. When she checked on how they were relating to Jim, she found that they were not perfect, but they had made a huge change. Creating the crisis made a difference in her family.

In order to create a crisis, a Big Girl must have courage and a strong belief that stagnant, unhealthy relationships do nothing. The status quo of underlying conflict is not a place of peace. Crisis has a way of blowing the cap off stuffed feelings. It may be hard to begin with, but often it can lead to productive dialogue. The truth is, there is nothing mature or Big-Girl-like in letting conflict continue to bubble right under the surface. Bringing the issue out in the open may be painful and may get an unexpectedly hostile result, but one thing is for sure: You cannot go back to business as usual.

If you find yourself in this situation and you are shaky about it, I recommend that you enlist the aid of a trusted counselor or Big-Girl friend who knows the situation and is willing to walk with you through it. I have done this as a counselor and also as a friend. It is scary to walk alone into a situation where you know there is going to be fire, but if you stick to the facts, focus on the desired outcome, and apply the other Big Girl behaviors outlined in this book, it is amazing what can happen. Creating crises really works when you want to be a Big Girl. With wisdom and a dash of bravery, it is a great way to move through. At the time, it may not feel as if peace will ever be possible, but if you deal in truth spoken with love, something will have to happen.

What If You Can't Resolve the Conflict?

If for some reason (and there can be many) you can't resolve the conflict between you and the other party, life goes on. Remember, God says *as far as it depends on you,* live at peace with everyone. If you have done all you know to do to bring a resolution, and it has failed, then you have to resolve things within yourself. It is important not to let the "poor me" or "guilty me" of self-pity bog you down. "As far as it depends on you" is as far as you can go!

Make sure you have made an honest effort to resolve the conflict. If you simply expect the other person to act exactly as you wish, you will never resolve it. If you are willing to be flexible and reasonable, there is a good chance you will come to agreeable terms. Maybe a little time and space will give you another opportunity.

The time will come when you will have to let the conflict go. I'll say it again: You can do everything in your power to resolve a problem, but if the other person doesn't want it resolved, it won't happen, and you shouldn't carry that burden around. This is the point where you must respond to God's command to "humble yourselves, therefore, under the mighty hand of God, that He may exalt you at the proper time, casting all your anxiety upon Him, because He cares for you" (1 Peter 5:6–7). When you have done everything you know to do, it is time to bow low before the Father and cast (which means "hurl deliberately") all of your cares to Him. He knows, He understands, and He cares. There is no better place to leave your problems.

Praying for God to bless the other person is a real Big-Girl thing to do. Ask Him to meet every need in her life and to draw her close to Himself. This prayer may merely be an action without desire at first, but when you do it, you will find yourself really meaning what you say.

Forgive the person with whom you have had a conflict. That doesn't let him off the hook, but it unhooks *you* from the situation. When you forgive, you give up your right to punish the other person, but you also send away the offense. When a Big Girl forgives, she follows the injunction in Ephesians 4:31–32: "Let all bitterness and wrath and anger and clamor and slander be put away from you, along with all malice. And be kind to one another, tender-hearted, forgiving each other, just as God in Christ also has forgiven you." When you forgive, it shows. Forgiving someone isn't just a matter of saying, "I have forgiven." It is a choice of your mind and heart that reveals itself in your behavior.

Resolving conflict is not an easy thing to do, but it does reflect the heart of God. That is why He "became flesh, and dwelt among us" (John 1:14). He wanted to resolve the conflict between mankind's sinfulness and His holiness. He knew that there was no way we could resolve that conflict on our own. We just didn't have it in us. So He sent His Son, Jesus Christ,

> who, although He existed in the form of God, did not regard equality with God a thing to be grasped, but emptied Himself, taking the form of a bond-servant, and being made in the likeness of men. And being found in appearance as a man, He humbled Himself by becoming obedient to the point of death, even death on a cross. (Philippians 2:6–8)

Through that cross, the conflict between man and God was resolved. If God went to such extreme measures to resolve our conflict with Him, how much more should we be determined that we will be committed to conflict resolution? It is His heart, and I believe He plants His will in the heart of every Big Girl who loves Him.

Nine

Stability for Big Girls in Crisis

Keeping Your Sanity in Insane Situations

I AM WRITING THIS CHAPTER in the middle of a crisis. The son of a very close friend has been in a grinding car wreck. His body has broken bones and smashed internal organs, and right now he is fighting pneumonia and hanging on to life. This is a crisis. As I have sat in the waiting room, seeing people come and go, hearing doctors' reports range from optimistic to pessimistic, I have been enrolled in the School for Big Girls in Crisis.

No matter where you are on the maturity scale, you will go through crises. That's life. Our lives *will* be interrupted and we *will* face suffering. There is no way to avoid it.

HOW BIG GIRLS FACE CRISIS

Here are some facts that I know are true no matter what. Each of us is knit together differently, and so our outward emotional responses to crisis may be quite varied, but read on to see what a mature response looks like.

BIG GIRLS DEAL WITH THE SITUATION

When a crisis happens, a Big Girl wants to see it for what it is. She doesn't minimize it or dramatize it. What is, is. She knows that seeing things as they are is the only way she can get a proper perspective. Pretending things are different than they are does her and the people she loves no good. I love the story of the widow of Zarepath. She was a Big Girl who dealt with crisis straight on.

> Later on the woman's son became sick. The sickness took a turn for the worse—and then he stopped breathing.
>
> The woman said to Elijah, "Why did you ever show up here in the first place—a holy man barging in, exposing my sins, and killing my son?"
>
> Elijah said, "Hand me your son." He then took him from her bosom, carried him up to the loft where he was staying, and laid him on his bed. Then he prayed, "O GOD, my God, why have you brought this terrible thing on this widow who has opened her home to me? Why have you killed her son?"
>
> Three times he stretched himself out full-length on the boy, praying with all his might, "GOD, my God, put breath back into this boy's body!" God listened to Elijah's prayer and put breath back into his body—he was alive! Elijah picked the boy up, carried him downstairs from the loft, and gave him to his mother. "Here's your son," said Elijah, "alive!"
>
> The woman said to Elijah, "I see it all now—you *are* a holy man. When you speak, God speaks—a true word!" (1 Kings 17:7–24 MSG)

Even if it is hard to wrap her mind around the crisis, a Big Girl does not want to be shielded from the truth.

BIG GIRLS UNDERSTAND THAT EVERYONE COPES WITH CRISIS UNIQUELY

Some people shut down. Some people talk, talk, talk. Some want to be distracted by a lot of people. Others want to be alone. A Big Girl knows that she has to be true to her way of dealing with things. Too often we can regret the way we have walked through a crisis because we allow other people to put their coping mechanisms on us. A young mother I know lost her child in a freak accident. Six months after his death, a well-meaning, albeit uninformed, woman at her church asked if she "had put closure on that awful event yet." The statement caused the mother to question whether her faith was really sure, because she had moments of grief and meltdown. When you are in a crisis, you have to do what is best for you. If it is your crisis, then how you handle it is your call.

BIG GIRLS GO WITH WHAT THEY KNOW

When you are in the middle of a crisis, speculation will rip away at your confidence. Wondering what the end result will be is often the weakest point in your battle. It is so natural to want to know what your situation will look like weeks down the road, but no one knows the future. This is where you have to stand on what you do know, and the best place to begin is to grab hold of what you know about God. You may not know anything for sure about your circumstances, but you do know many things for sure about the God who rules over your circumstances.

- *He will never leave you.* "I WILL NEVER DESERT YOU, NOR WILL I EVER FORSAKE YOU" (Hebrews 13:5).

- *He will never allow you to go through more than you can bear.*

"No test or temptation that comes your way is beyond the course of what others have had to face. All you need to remember is that God will never let you down; he'll never let you be pushed past your limit; he'll always be there to help you come through it" (1 Corinthians 10:13 MSG).

- *He will never allow you to be separated from His love.* There is nothing that can come between you and your Maker. "For I am convinced that neither death nor life, neither angels nor demons, neither the present nor the future, nor any powers, neither height nor depth, nor anything else in all creation, will be able to separate us from the love of God that is in Christ Jesus our Lord" (Romans 8:38 NIV).

- *He is intimately involved in your life and with those you love.* "The LORD will accomplish what concerns me; Your lovingkindness, O LORD, is everlasting; do not forsake the works of Your hands" (Psalm 138:8).

- *He knows exactly what you are feeling, and He is touched by what you feel.* "We do not have a high priest who is unable to sympathize with our weaknesses, but we have one who has been tempted in every way, just as we are—yet was without sin. Let us then approach the throne of grace with confidence, so that we may receive mercy and find grace to help us in our time of need" (Hebrews 4:15–16 NIV).

- *He has plans for you that include a future and a hope.* "'For I know the plans I have for you,' declares the LORD, 'plans to prosper you and not to harm you, plans to give you hope and a future'" (Jeremiah 29:11 NIV).

- *There are things going on in the unseen realm that you cannot know.* "For momentary, light affliction is producing for us an eternal weight of glory far beyond all comparison, while we look not at the things which are seen, but at the things which are not seen; for the things which are seen are temporal, but the things which are not seen are eternal" (2 Corinthians 4:17–18).

- *The Spirit of God is praying for you.* "For we do not know how to pray as we should, but the Spirit Himself intercedes for us with groanings too deep for words; and He who searches the hearts knows what the mind of the Spirit is, because He intercedes for the saints according to the will of God" (Romans 8:26–27).

- *There are angels attending you.* "For He will give His angels charge concerning you, to guard you in all your ways. They will bear you up in their hands, that you do not strike your foot against a stone" (Psalm 91:11–12).

- *His love is based on His will to love, not on your performance.* "We love, because He first loved us" (1 John 4:19).

- *Heaven is the goal. Earth is not heaven.* "For our citizenship is in heaven, from which also we eagerly wait for a Savior, the Lord Jesus Christ; who will transform the body of our humble state into conformity with the body of His glory, by the exertion of the power that He has even to subject all things to Himself" (Philippians 3:20–21).

Big-Girl Truth to Live By:

The best place to begin is to grab hold of what you know about God.

One woman who lost her father unexpectedly to a heart attack—this after three close friends and family members died in the previous year—

wrote the following message to her prayer partners. Her perspective provides a wonderful example of a Big Girl embracing crisis and "going with what she knows" about the Lord's strength:

By now you have all heard the sad news that my dad passed away. I must say I am completely shocked, and it will take some time to really accept that he is gone. I have to say, since all of you know the recent sorrow of losing Susan (and before that Katie and Alison) and my mom's scheduled surgery for Friday, I am a bit on overload. I know I will not make it (and have not made it thus far) without your prayers. I have had countless conversations with people who interacted with my dad, and have been blessed by his life, which is so comforting.

The memorial service is Saturday. Please pray for supernatural strength for all of us. Dad put me "in charge" of all the arrangements, . . . but I know God will give me the grace to take one thing at a time. I have cried *many* tears, and will continue to. There are several family members and friends who don't know the Lord yet, so is is my greatest desire, and I know my dad's too, that his life and death would bring them to the Lord.

Thank you for your prayers, and I know that you will continue to pray for us, including my mom's surgery. (Believe me, I am trusting Him to take care of her, too.)

In the midst of all this in my personal life, I cannot even touch the latest tragedy of the shuttle explosion [January 2003]. God knows, and somehow our nation will hopefully cry out to Him in the midst of this loss. For me, I can barely handle the personal loss, and yet I know He will carry us through the corporate loss as well. He is very good.

BIG GIRLS KNOW EVERY CRISIS HAS AN END

First Peter 1:6 is a special comfort when you are in the middle of a crisis. It was penned by the apostle Peter, who was writing to people whose lives were in one big upheaval. They were Christians under Roman rule who were daily confronted with the possibility of a crisis, like being snatched off the street and hung on a lamppost to burn for being a Christian. They lived in terrifying times, and the trials were horrific. So imagine the comfort when Peter wrote, "In this [speaking of the salvation which they had been given] you greatly rejoice, even though now for a little while, if necessary, you have been distressed by various trials." In the original translation, that phrase "for a little while," is "how little, how little." Your crisis may seem long, but compared to eternity, you know it has a limit. It will not last forever. Big Girls remind themselves that every crisis has a beginning and an end.

WHEN IT IS NOT YOUR CRISIS

One of the special things about being a Big Girl is having the confidence to be able to stand by people you know and love in their crises. As a young woman, I hated going to a hospital room or a funeral home, because I really did not know what to say. I would never call or visit, because I

> **Big-Girl Truth to Live By:**
>
> *Big Girls remind themselves that every crisis has a beginning and an end.*

didn't want to interfere in the lives of people who were in crisis. Now I realize that we need each other when our worlds have been turned upside down. Big Girls know what is needed and make themselves available to give it. If they don't know, they ask. Little Girls usually spend valuable time guessing what is needed. They wonder what they should do and so, frequently, they miss it!

Here are some pointers for being a Big Girl in someone else's crisis. (You may already be able to add some ideas from your own experience. If so, jot them down at the end of the chapter. You never know when you might be called upon to help someone.)

BIG GIRLS UNDERSTAND BOUNDARIES

The closer you are to a person in crisis, the greater your permission to be involved.

You may not be close enough to do housekeeping after a death in the family, but you may be close enough to coordinate meals. Big Girls will not assume. They will ask, "Would it be helpful if I did this or that?" Sometimes too much help can be a burden.

Being close is based on experience, not necessarily a blood tie. Just because you are part of the family does not mean that you automatically have the right or permission to come into a situation and take over. Big Girls recognize this and are willing to give deference to the wishes of the person in crisis. Big Girls think, *Do unto others as you would have them do unto you.* Therefore, they think before they assume a relationship.

BIG GIRLS UNDERSTAND THAT THE CRISIS IS NOT ABOUT THEM

One of my pet Big-Girl peeves is Little Girls who arrive where there is trouble and, before you know it, they make the situation all about them. I can't count how many times I have heard inane comments in hospitals and funeral homes. Usually the people making them are so totally self-absorbed they don't even realize how inappropriate and uncaring they are. One of the most inappropriate statements I have heard was at the death of a friend's son. The people who had come to comfort were not there long before they took out their grandchildren's pictures and began to show them around the room, saying, "I don't know what we would do if something happened to one of our children." *Oh, please,* my Big-Girl heart protested. *Do you think these people volunteered for this tragedy? This is not about YOU!*

Big Girls come and go quietly when there is trouble. They can serve in difficulties with no need to explain the situation or put themselves in the middle of it. They know that sometimes, the less said the better. "I'm sorry," "I love you," or just silently sitting and holding a friend's hand may be quite enough.

BIG GIRLS UNDERSTAND TIME LIMITS

People in crisis grow weary quickly. The demands on their emotional and physical abilities exceed what is usually required. Big Girls know that a quick visit, a card in the mail, or a vase of flowers will go miles toward letting the person know they are loved. Long visits where the person in crisis has to think of something to say and entertain the visitors are inappropriate.

Unless invited to stay longer, Big Girls observe the five-minute limit and get on with it! Part of knowing time limits seems to be an innate thing with Big Girls. They develop awareness of others that allows them to be sensitive to situations everywhere. If there are several visitors, make your stay very brief. If someone has come from out of town to visit the person in crisis, cut your visit short to allow them time. Bring a treat that you know the family might enjoy when you come. I've noticed that often Little Girls come with good intentions, but they don't know when to leave with good intentions. A short visit is better than a long one.

It is as much an art to know when to leave as it is to know when to come. If the people you are visiting want you to stay, they will say so. If not, assume a quick visit it enough.

Good questions to ask when you are ready to leave are,

- "Can I get you anything?"

- "I'll go now, but I'll be back another day if that is all right."

- "If you want me to pick up anything for you, here's my number."

Making yourself available is always welcomed. The focus stays on the situation and the people in it rather than on you.

When I am in that kind of situation, especially when there has been a death, I remember these very poignant words written by Joseph Bayley in his book *The Last Thing We Talk About*.

I was sitting, torn by grief. Someone came and talked to me of God's dealings, of why it happened, of hope beyond the grave. He talked constantly. He said things I knew were true.

I was unmoved, except to wish he'd go away. He finally did.

Another came and sat beside me. He didn't talk. He didn't ask leading questions. He just sat beside me for an hour and more, listened when I said something, answered briefly, prayed, simply left.

I was moved. I was comforted. I hated to see him go.[1]

BIG GIRLS DON'T TRY TO
ANSWER EVERY QUESTION

When a crisis hits, inevitably there will be questions—questions about why the crisis happened, what God is trying to say, why the victim is going through this, and what the big picture could possibly be. The questions go on and on, but Big Girls know they don't have all the answers, so they don't stumble off into areas where only God can respond. It is pure folly, for instance, to try to tell someone why she is in a crisis, even if you think you know why, because in reality, you don't know. It may seem to you that there is a logical reason for the trouble, but God may have a very illogical reason, or at least a reason that looks illogical to you.

I think of that passage in John 9 where Jesus' disciples observed a man who had been born blind from birth. The disciples assumed they knew why this man experienced the crisis of being born blind. "His disciples asked him, 'Rabbi, who sinned, this man or his parents, that he was born blind?'" (John 9:2 NIV). They had it all figured out: No baby would be born blind unless his parents had sinned. All illness and defect is a result of someone's sin, right? Well, Jesus threw them a curve. "'Neither this man nor his parents sinned,' said Jesus, 'but this happened so that that the work of God might be displayed in his life'" (v. 3).

I hear you: "Huh? Do you mean to tell me, Jan, that sometimes only God can give an answer because He is the only One who knows the real reason?" Absolutely. And here's another thing you can be absolutely sure about: God has no obligation to explain *why* when we want the answer.

So what do you do as a Big Girl when the questions come up? I am a firm believer that not every question requires an answer. Don't meddle with what you don't know. There is nothing wrong with saying, "I don't know," and leave it at that. Some of us have trouble with this. We feel we have to come up with an answer when God has not given one. Consequently, we sometimes offer answers that can leave behind a trail of guilt and confusion that was totally unnecessary.

THE GOOD SIDE OF CRISIS

One of the very priceless residuals you bring out of crisis is the realization that you made it through. And since you made it through this event, you can make it through the next one. You realize that you may have taken some tough blows, but you are a survivor, a fighter, and you will not go down for the count.

The vigil I am keeping at this point is with a friend who has proven she is the ultimate Big Girl. She will survive. Her name is Deborah Klassen. Her son Ryan is twenty-seven years old. When he was nine years old he was diagnosed with a rare form of cancer in his sinus. He went through extensive surgery, chemotherapy, and radiation. He lived. He was facially disfigured and has had to deal with a lot of issues that come into a life when everything changes. Now he is fighting to survive one more time.

His condition is so tenuous; his pain is so horrible; his future is so uncertain. Once again, his mother and father are at his bedside facing a crisis they didn't ask for, nor did they expect. But their faith is shining like gold. They are devastated, bewildered, and torn apart by what has happened to their son. But this one thing they know: The same God who got them through when he was nine will get them through this time as well. No matter which way it goes, whether their son lives or dies, they will make it. How do I know? Track records are amazing things. When you have made it through once, chances are you will make it through again. (At the time I am writing these last pages, the good news is that Ryan survived. He has an altered life and a long rehabilitation, but he is alive and we are grateful!)

Another benefit of crisis is that it brings perspective. Going through a crisis is like taking a long journey. If you want to travel with the greatest ease, you don't take any excess baggage with you. When you are in a crisis, emotional baggage has to be set aside. Your emotions will be on high alert anyway. Difficult people in your life, raw feelings, old hurts, leftover anger, and hostilities all have to be put aside. There will be another day for dealing with those. When you are in a crisis, you really need to narrow your focus and simplify your world. Only a few things are needed: rest, food, quiet, the Word of God, and time to think and pray. You need a few good friends or trusted family willing to come along-side you, and some hope. That's about it. Actually, does life require anything else?

Big Girls know that life on the planet isn't easy. Crises come into your world, usually with no warning. Big Girls know they have a big God who knows the big picture, who has a big plan, and who is willing to comfort them in a really big way. Big Girls allow themselves to go into crisis mode when required, and when the crisis is over, they gradually return to a more normal routine.

Little Girls are like toddlers who see everything that displeases them as a tragedy. They move from one crisis to another, rarely taking a break to live normally. Some of them really don't feel they are living if they aren't having a crisis.

Big Girls know that being in a crisis isn't really living. They're simply dealing with immediate, heavy circumstances with grace that is given for the moment. They know the reality of "dying grace for dying days," as my former pastor Wayne Barber says. But they don't stretch the grace of God by living in crisis mode when they are not in crisis, expecting His comforting presence to get them through just because they keep their lives in a turmoil. They also don't stretch the grace of their friends. I know of a woman who lives like this, to the point of dishonoring her agreements, contractual and otherwise, with other people. The most important things in her life are the things that are important to *her*, and she expects everyone to accommodate her "needs." It's hard to be gracious to someone in perpetual crisis after a time.

Crises are hard, but they are memorable and carry many valuable lessons for those who are open to learning. Where would we be if we never faced the impossibility and questions that crises bring? Where would we be if God didn't push back the curtain of time and remind us that no matter what we are going through, there is a God and we are not Him? God gives us His words that bring comfort in the darkest night.

And not only that, but we also glory in tribulations, knowing that tribulation produces perseverance; and perseverance, character; and character, hope. Now hope does not disappoint, because the love of God has been poured out in our hearts by the Holy Spirit who was given to us. (Romans 5:3–5 NKJV)

God knows about our crises. He is present in the middle of them, and in His great love for us, He always offers hope. So the next time a crisis hits, grab hold of His hope and His love, and refuse to let go.

Ten

Leaving a Godly Legacy

Passing on the Treasure of Being a Big Girl

O LD AGE ISN'T FOR SISSIES."[1] But it isn't for Little Girls either. As a woman finds her years of living piling up, she can use them to create a self-centered, miserable demeanor or a lovely, rich legacy of wisdom and wonder to pass on to the Big Girls in process in her life.

When you meet an older Big Girl, you have met a treasure. She has been a work in progress for a lot of years, and when she reaches the last few decades of her life, the work becomes more complete and beautiful.

I never knew my grandmothers. One died when she was thirty-six years old due to complications from the birth of her tenth child. The other lived far away, and although I met her, I never really knew her. So the treasures of wisdom passed down to me in my family have come primarily from my mother and her sisters. What a grand bunch of Big Girls they are: positive, kind, caring, and fun. They are elderly now, but the spirit of the Big Girl lives stronger than ever within them. Some of them have lost their lifelong companions; some have gone through their own personal illnesses; but still they stand strong, optimistic, and full of hope.

Of course, senior Big Girls haven't been mature all their lives. They would be the first to smile and say, "I had to grow and go through some of the tough courses of life to get to the golden years." Do you ever wonder why the latter years of life are called golden? I'm not sure of all the reasons, but this I do know: Gold must go through the fire to be refined and purified from all contaminants before it can be labeled "pure."

> **Big-Girl Truth to Live By:**
>
> *In the golden years, the fruit of a Big Girl's life becomes increasingly beautiful and priceless.*

Big Girls, too, have to go through the refiner's fire before they can become all they were designed to be. It is never fun to be in the fire. Periods of testing are never something a Big Girl in her right mind goes looking for, but when she is in there, something special happens—something only the fire can do. The testing by fire that God allows in all of our lives is designed to bring good out of us. In fact, the apostle Peter says it all:

> In this you greatly rejoice, even though now for a little while, if necessary, you have been distressed by various trials, that the proof of your faith, being more precious than gold which is perishable, even though tested by fire, may be found to result in praise and glory and honor at the revelation of Jesus Christ. (1 Peter 1:6–7)

That Greek word for "tested," *dokimazo*, is a great word. It means "something good is expected." This kind of test is designed "to prove what is good in us or to make us good." This word is never used of Satan, "since he never wants us to experience God's approval. He always tempts *(periazei)* us, with the intent to make us fall."[2]

Any test you go through in life is part of the refining, purifying, beautifying work of God. That truth is part of the legacy that Big Girls can pass on to Big Girls in process. When these growing women are in the fiery valleys of life's experiences, Big Girls come alongside them and say, "You can make it. I've walked through that valley, and you can too."

The gifts that senior Big Girls have to give other women contrast starkly with the hand-me-downs from old Little Girls who never understood that life is to be lived well, even in the fires. Little Girls are still so self-absorbed when they get older they can't see the work of the fire. They know only that it's hot and undesirable.

Old Little Girls also have a tendency to whine a lot and to give organ recitals. You know the tune. Their anthem is the singsong litany of all that is wrong, and they sing it best when there is an audience:

> My knees, my shoulders, my gaseous complaints.
> My sleep deprivation, my disgust with the saints.
> I'm old and cranky, oh what should I do?
> If I can't figure it out, I'll just dump it on you![3]

You have probably heard that ditty or something like it and thought, *God preserve me from myself when I grow old!*

NAMING OUR TREASURES

What treasures can you pass along to other growing women? Big Girls along the way have woven their lives into your Big-Girl legacy, though you may have been unaware of it. It's easy to take this for granted. As you embrace those treasures, however, they become part of you.

When I consider the legacy that has been passed on to me, I think, *I had better not start to whine. Mother and the aunties will be on me like white on rice.* They are Big Girls who have given me priceless gifts. It is my duty now to treasure them and pass them on. What follows is a list of some of the treasures I have received from other Big Girls in my life. I hope it will inspire you to list your own and be grateful. Thank the Big Girls who are still here, and thank God for allowing them and those who have gone on before to be in your life. What a privilege I've had to rub shoulders with Big Girls like these:

- My mother: "You can do whatever you set out to do. I expect the best."

- My aunts: "All for one and one for all," with apologies to the Three Musketeers! Overcoming adversity together is easier than trying to do it alone.

- Edna Woofter: "I believe in you." "God is faithful."

- Arvine Bell: "Remember who you are, where you're from, and what you represent."

- Johnnie Armstrong: "Friends are always friends." "Keep your tennis shoes clean."

- Kay Arthur: "Is that biblical?" "I admire you."

- Dr. Marie Chapian: "Tell yourself the truth."

- Mary Graham: "Lead with love; it always works."

- Luci Swindoll: "Embrace life; it is to be lived."

- Marilyn Meberg: "Alone does not mean lonely."

- Sheila Walsh: "Passion! Keep the passion."

- Thelma Wells: "You can 'bee!'"

- Patsy Clairmont: "You are ten feet tall even when you feel very small."

- Nicole Johnson: "Look for the message beyond the obvious."

- Beth Moore: "God is crazy about you."

- Babbie Mason: "When you can't trace His hand, trust His heart."

- Sandy Smith: "I'm praying, praying, praying."

OF FRIENDS AND MENTORS

Big Girls pass truth on to Big Girls in process. That's how our tribe increases!

I've thought a lot about passing on the Big-Girl legacy to my two daughters-in-law and my three granddaughters. While my three sons were growing up, it never occurred to me that I would have the chance to pass anything on to them except my love and example as a mother. When they married, I wondered if it would be possible for me as a mother-in-law to pass anything on to the girls my boys had chosen. (If you are a mother-in-law, you probably have wondered the same thing.) Having grown to know them and establishing that we really like and love each other, I thought they might appreciate what I had to share, but we had never talked about it, so I didn't know for sure.

I had a conversation with "my girls" about writing this book and asked them what they as Big Girls in process might want me to pass on to them. They were quick to tell me: "We want your friendship, and we want to learn from you." That was music to my ears. Their response was what I had hoped for all along, and it was affirming to hear it from their lips.

Being friends is the first step to passing treasures on to a Big Girl in process. You can't pass on truth and wisdom and insight and love in a vacuum. You have to take the time to get to know the Big Girls who want to learn. Before they can learn from you, they need to be loved by you.

> **Big-Girl Truth to Live By:**
>
> *Truth and wisdom and insight and love can't be passed on in a vacuum.*

Mentoring is a hot topic these days. There is a great hunger among younger women for the kind of relationship that will encourage them to grow and learn to be Big Girls (whether they call it that or not). Many organized mentoring attempts fizzle after a few months because friendships aren't established first. If a Big Girl and a Big Girl in progress do not have a mutual care and respect for each other, then there is little they can comfortably discuss and share. If, however, the relationship is anchored in friendship first, then the exchange of truth and wisdom will be a natural part of its development.

The truth is that Big Girls usually congregate with other Big Girls. Naturally, they have similar interests and concerns and are often of similar age. So in order for mature Big Girls to pass on the Big-Girl legacy, they might find the need to step out of their comfort zones in order to associate with Little Girls who want to be Big Girls in progress.

If you are in a church, you can find opportunities to connect with younger women. I think it is a lovely idea for the older women to work in the nursery several times a year. That frees up young women to participate in the church services and not have to stay in the nursery so often, but it also gives a point of contact between them. When Big Girls serve Little Girls, they set the stage to share life in a more intimate way. Too often, age is an excuse to sit back and "let the young folks do it." When older Big Girls step up to the plate to serve and share their life with Big Girls in process, everyone wins.

Neighborhood Bible studies are also a wonderful way for mature Big Girls and Big Girls in process to come together on common ground. Mature Big Girls can host a Bible study with a universal topic or one that appeals specifically to younger women. You might even use this book to start.

If you have it in you to be a mentor, there are Big Girls in process who want what you have to share. They will have to trust you, however, not to constantly revert to the old days. They want to know that you can give them wisdom that fits in the twenty-first century and that you will be authentic and accepting of who and where they are. God has an amazing way of connecting the dots in your life to put you in touch with the people He means for you to meet. Talk to Him and then be open, be alert, be available.

Several women in my life are Big Girls in process or mature Big Girls. In many instances, I have been just one of several women in their lives who has said, "Here's what I have to share. Take it and run with it." One group of women I know has amazed me beyond belief. We started meeting several years ago when each of them was going through a crisis. I was working as a family counselor and had seen each of them individually. They were looking for ways to cope, to grow, to be free. Knowing that there is much value in the group dynamic and believing that these women would grow if the soil was watered just a little bit, I called the group together to meet on a weekly basis. So we began to meet. We developed relationships, shared our lives and the wisdom God had given us, and today they are an incredible group. Each one has become a bona fide Big Girl. They are functioning with grace and strength and honor and are passing on their treasures to others in their lives. And just for the record, we get together occasionally now just to love each other and bask in our corporate "Big Girlness." We don't have to meet for support anymore. We just choose to get together for the joy of the journey, and we love it.

I am in awe of the Big Girls God has allowed me to know and love. It is a privilege to be part of their lives. I really believe that this is the modern-day example of Titus 2:3–5:

> Older women likewise are to be reverent in their behavior, not malicious gossips, nor enslaved to much wine, teaching what is good, so that they may encourage the young women to love their husbands, to love their children, to be sensible, pure, workers at home, kind, being subject to their own husbands, so that the word of God will not be dishonored.

Following are some treasures of the legacy a Big-Girl friend and mentor would want to pass on.

THE TREASURE OF APPROPRIATE BEHAVIOR

Big Girls in progress learn what is appropriate by seeing it modeled for them. Big Girls are quality material, and they exemplify quality in their behavior. They live their lives in such a way that they can say without hesitation, "Follow me." They have themselves under control.

A Big Girl keeps her tongue in check. We usually think about profanity or malicious gossip as being the big issues in this category, but sometimes talking too much about nothing is a dead giveaway that a Little Girl's tongue is out of control. I have often sat on the plane and listened to women talk and talk and talk until surely there could be nothing left to talk about. It's a long way from Atlanta to Los Angeles when a Little Girl is talking, talking, talking. Telling everything you know about every topic can leave others with nothing to say.

A Big Girl's manners often are revealed through the graciousness in her words. Big Girls know that "good manners look good on anybody" and so they make an effort to be mannerly, gracious, and kind. That becomes natural for a true Big Girl. Part of that gracious, mannerly spirit involves asking questions that indicate interest in the Big Girl in process. Bona fide Big Girls know that expressing an interest is a healthy way to build a bond. Nosey, invasive questions are inappropriate, but questions such as, "Tell me about your family," or, "Tell me about your job" or "your church" or "your favorite thing to do" all are appropriate and can be answered in whatever depth the other person wants to go. Giving practical, universal, up-to-date tips to someone who is younger is a great way to start building that all-important relationship. If "what was" is applicable to "what is" now, that can be a great place to connect.

I remember talking to one of my favorite Big Girls when I was much younger and very much in process. She had raised a family of four and was a gracious, lovely woman. One day in casual conversation, I was talking about how hard it was to keep the house picked up with three little boys under foot. I had no expectation that she could do anything about it, but she caught my attention when she mentioned that she made a habit of picking up anything that was out of place before she went to bed. She remarked that it only took a few minutes, and it was so much easier to get up to a tidy house in the morning. From that day forward, I made it a habit to put things back in their places before I go to bed. She taught me something important by her example as well as her words. She showed me how picking things up is one way to love my husband and train my children. She always spoke of her love for her husband and how she valued him. She painted the picture of a Big Girl by the way she showed me that particular slice of life.

The Treasure of Wisdom

Big Girls never know what wisdom they are passing on to the Big Girls in process. I was working in the nursery one day with a mature Big Girl who rocked a toddler to sleep while I played with a child on the floor. This Big Girl was a friend. She had a grown son who was a prodigal. He was away from home and her heart was broken. As she rocked the toddler, she said, "I would give anything to have John back at this point." Then she said, "When my husband used to correct him, I would always step in. I didn't let him correct his own son. Oh, how I wished I had let Jack handle John. It takes the harshness of a man to raise a man." She bowed her head toward the baby, held him, and rocked him, and I knew that I had heard something very important for my life. I was a Big Girl in process who was the mother of three very young sons. Like any mother, I wanted to protect them when they got themselves in trouble. The words that this older Big Girl spoke that day changed the way I dealt with my boys. When I wanted to protest that Charlie was being a little strict, I always remembered, "It takes the harshness of a man to raise a man." Of course, wisdom says you don't tolerate abuse, but there is wisdom in her observation that the strength and firmness of man is necessary for the formation of his sons.

Knowledge is a wonderful thing, but it can be reduced to a real stumbling block if "smarts" is all you have. You have to have wisdom to make knowledge acceptable.

I love what Proverbs says about wisdom:

> Make your ear attentive to wisdom,
> Incline your heart to understanding;
> For if you cry for discernment,
> Lift your voice for understanding;
> If you seek her as silver
> And search for her as for hidden treasures;
> Then you will discern the fear of the LORD
> And discover the knowledge of God.
> For the LORD gives wisdom;
> From His mouth come knowledge and understanding.
> He stores up sound wisdom for the upright;
> He is a shield to those who walk in integrity,
> Guarding the paths of justice,
> And He preserves the way of His godly ones.
> Then you will discern righteousness and justice
> And equity and every good course. (Proverbs 2:2–9)

I believe maturing Big Girls play a huge role in making wisdom look appealing. Unless Big Girls in process see the value of the pursuit of wisdom, it just doesn't make sense. Seeing someone who has gone after wisdom and who lives wisely is the biggest entice-ment for the growing Big Girl to stay strongly in pursuit.

Marge Caldwell is a woman whom many Big Girls can credit with being that woman of wisdom who made the difference in their lives. She has taught and mentored women for years. Giving them the knowledge that a great Bible teacher can give, she has also provided the practical wisdom that, when applied, turns Little Girls into Big Girls.

Popular Bible teacher Beth Moore credits Marge with much of the practical wisdom that has enabled her to be who she is today. Beth is a Big Girl who received the legacy from Marge and is faithfully passing it on to those who desire to live their lives with God to the fullest as the Big Girls He created them to be.

A Note to Big Girls in Process

Almost everyone has access to wise Big Girls in her realm of acquaintances. If you are a Big Girl in process who wants to have a mentor, look for someone you admire. Look at how she lives her life and handles her relationships, then ask her if she would be available to spend some time with you.

If you just don't know of any, you may have to look for a Big Girl among all the wonderful books that are available. In this day and time, no one can say, "There are no Big Girls I can learn from. I have no one from whom to receive that legacy!"

One of the people who has made me want to pursue wisdom and be a Big Girl is a woman I never met, but I have felt very close to her for many years. I cannot read her books and fail to know I have been in the presence of a Big Girl. Amy Carmichael is her name. She went to be with the Lord close to fifty years ago, but her life and the wisdom by which she lived have deeply, profoundly impacted me.

Amy Carmichael was a missionary to India for fifty years. She dedicated her life to rescuing babies and children from the ravages of Hindu temple prostitution. As far as she knew, that was the way she would spend her life. She loved her work and was wonderful at it. Little did she know that God had other plans for her life that would expand her impact far beyond what she could imagine.

This is her story:

There was a day for me—October 24—when I stood among three other happy people in Joyous City outside the door of the house we'd rented for the missions work there—which we'd found locked. We wondered what we should do. The old man who had charge of the key was not there, and the key was not to be found.

We stood for a long time in the swiftly gathering twilight, ready to turn contentedly toward home if we could not get in. Just then another old man hurried up, the huge key of his own courtyard door in his hand. "This may open it," he said hopefully.

There was a moment's fumbling. The door opened. We went in. . . .

What if the old man had not rushed up at the last moment with the key? What if the key had not worked? There was a pit dug, where no pit was supposed to be. And for me, a crippling fall. [A nightsoil pit was dug in the front room. This was unheard of and unexpected.]

The confused rollings and wheels of "second causes" do not help much here—or anywhere. The Lord allowed it. Therefore, so far as we are concerned, He did it. And all that He does is good. . . .

On October 6, eighteen days before, a member of our fellowship was at home in London. In a time of prayer, he was suddenly caused to feel that danger was threatening me. He prayed, not the easy prayer of the unconcerned, but the intense prayer of one greatly burdened. A sense of fear tried to overwhelm him, as of a terror by night. He continued on until peace came, and he knew that his prayer was heard. . . .

Should we have said that prayer was *not* answered? It is a petty view of our Father's love and wisdom which demands or expects an answer according to our desires, apart from His wisdom.

We see hardly one inch of the narrow lane of time. To our God, eternity lies open as a meadow. It must seem strange to the heavenly people, who have reached the beautiful End, that you and I should ever question what Love allows to be, or that we ever call prayer "unanswered" when it is not what we expect.

. . . Isn't *no* an answer?

. . . Isn't *heaven* an answer?[4]

The irony of Amy Carmichael's life is that she touched more lives in the twenty years after her fall than she ever could have influenced before it happened. She became bedfast and ended up spending her days writing. She wrote letters to the young people who were part of the work that she had established. She wrote for her own personal devotions. Today, because so much of what she wrote has been published, we are the richer. She was a Big Girl who did not allow her life circumstances to stop her from being effective. She passed the legacy on to some whom she knew would run with it, but her writings took her wisdom even to people she would never know on this earth.

Having read Miss Carmichael's writings, I can look back on my life and see her impact on it. I see truths I believe and live by, but I often wonder, *Where did I learn that? How did I know to think that?* Many of the Big Girl qualities in my life have come from a woman I never knew personally but will no doubt recognize when we meet in the "beautiful End." Thank you, Amy, for being a Big Girl through it all.

LOOKING FORWARD TO "AFTER A WHILE"

I recently held a "Girl Cousins' Spend-the-Night" for my grand-daughters. I did this because I wanted them to have fun, but more than that I am keenly aware that each of them is a growing little girl with Big-Girl potential. They are created with gifts, possibil-ities, and length of days that only God knows. I am a significant Big Girl in their lives, and it is my privilege to give them all that I can so that someday they will know the joy of being grown up and really liking it! Big Girls love being Big Girls, because with that position comes wonderful privileges that Little Girls never know. Passing on the legacy is one of them.

I want my granddaughters to consider that being a Big Girl who loves God is the very best thing they can aspire to in their lives. I want their vision of a being a capable woman who lives contentedly and peacefully to be far stronger than the little-girl dreams of being a Barbie princess in a mythological kingdom, waiting for a Ken who may never come along. I want my little girls to know that life is wonderful because it is a gift. Whether they make their journey married or single, I want them to know God loves them and that He is intimately involved in every aspect of their being. I want my little girls to grow into Big Girls who understand the words of this familiar poem titled "After a While," which I have loved for years. These are the words of a Big Girl.

> After a while you learn the subtle difference between
>   holding a hand and chaining a soul,
>   and you learn that love doesn't mean leaning

and company doesn't mean security.
After a while you begin to learn that kisses aren't contracts
　　and presents aren't promises,
　　　and you begin to accept your defeats
　　　with your head up and your eyes open,
　　　with the grace of an adult, not the grief of a child.
After a while you learn to build your roads on today because
　　tomorrow's grounds are too uncertain for plans.
After a while you learn that even sunshine burns
　　if you get too much. So plant your garden
　　and decorate your own soul instead of waiting
　　for someone to bring you flowers.
　　And you learn that you really can endure,
　　. . . that you really are strong
　　. . . and you really do have worth.[5]

After a while, you learn that being a Big Girl is something you don't want to miss. It is a place of grown-up joy and empowerment. It is a position planned by God for you to inhabit. It is why you lived through the years of being a Little Girl so you could emerge full grown, fully alive, and equipped to face life with extraordinary skill.

If you have read this book and are embracing the title of Big Girl for yourself, I applaud you. You have a great deal to look forward to, a great deal to experience, and you will have even more to pass on to the Little Girls you love.

May you always know how much God loves His girls and how great His heart is toward you!

Notes

CHAPTER TWO

1. Melvin E. Dieter and Hallie Dieter, *God Is Enough* (Grand Rapids: Zondervan Publishing House, 1986), 5–6.

2. Hannah Whitall Smith, *The God of All Comfort and the Secret of His Comforting* (London: James Nisbet & Co., Limited, 1906), 155–6.

CHAPTER THREE

1. Hannah Whitall Smith, "Giving Up and Growing Up," quoted in Melvin E. Dieter, 109.

CHAPTER FOUR

1. For a complete discussion on codependency, see my book *Please Don't Say You Need Me: Biblical Answers for Co-Dependency* (Grand Rapids: Zondervan, 1989).

CHAPTER SEVEN

1. F. R. Andrew, "Seven Words from the Cross," quoted in *Forever Friends* (Nashville: Thomas Nelson, 1994), n.p.

2. George Eliot, quoted in W. H. Auden and Louis Kronenberger, ed., *The Treasure Chest* (New York: HarperCollins, 1965), 97.

3. William Penn, quoted in *The Treasure Chest*, 96.

CHAPTER EIGHT

1. Dave Burchett, *When Bad Christians Happen to Good People* (Colorado Springs: WaterBrook Press, 2002), 2.

CHAPTER NINE

1. Joseph Bayley, *The Last Thing We Talk About*. Colorado Springs: Chariot Family Publishers, a Division of Cook Communications, 1992.

CHAPTER TEN

1. Charles R. Swindoll, *Moses* (W Publishing Group, Nashville, TN, 2001), 253.

2. *The Hebrew-Greek Key Study Bible*, ed. Spiros Zodhiates (Chattanooga, TN: AMG Publishers, 1990), 1826.

3. *The Hebrew-Greek Key Study Bible*, ed. Spiros Zodhiates (Chattanooga, TN: AMG Publishers, 1990), 1826.

4. Amy Carmichael, from "Rose from Brier," quoted in *You Are My Hiding Place*, ed. David Hazard (Minneapolis: Bethany House Publishers, 1991) 149–150.

5. "After a While." Author unknown.

Reader's Guide

How To Use the Reader's Guide

There is nothing like getting together with girlfriends to discuss a point of mutual interest. I can assure you that once you have read *Big Girls Don't Whine,* you and your friends (and maybe even some women you have just met) will have discussion material for a long time. That's the way Big Girls are—we grab hold of truth and ride it to the farthest destination.

I encourage you to think through these life-changing principles and then have a great time discussing them with other women in your group. You will discover things about yourself, your relationship style and your spiritual connection that will amaze you, thrill you and maybe even jolt you, but this one thing I can assure you: You will never be the same again.

The questions are set up for Personal Reflection and Group Discussion. I think it's a great exercise in *processing* to do some personal reflection before you come together with your group. If you have thought things through on your own ahead of time, then your discussion will be richer. You won't be reacting to the questions but rather responding out of thoughtful pre-consideration.

As you work through your personal reflections and then go to your group discussion, there will be thoughts and quotes you will want to record. Why not get yourself a little notebook for such musings and call it your Big Girl Journal. I think you will be amazed to see your thinking change as you go through this process. So, be sure to date the entries so you can see the changing *you* emerge!

I encourage you to keep the group discussions positive. If you share shortcomings and areas of needed growth, make sure they are *your* areas of need, not your husband's or children's. This is about *you* changing, growing up and moving on. This is a Big Girl thing. Too often, when we see a need, we see it as belonging to the challenging people in our lives. To see our own needs, to deal with them and to alter our behavior is huge. It is really Big Girl! (This doesn't mean that the challenging people in our lives don't have needs. It does mean we aren't their *fixers*. We can only fix ourselves).

So, Big Girl, go for it! Make the most of this journey with other Big Girls who want to discover and live in the wonderful gift of the *Life God Intends*. What a treasure it is. Don't miss it!

INTRODUCTION:
FINDING THE TREASURE WITHIN

Personal Reflection

1. If you could make it happen right this minute, what would the Big Girl inside you look like?
2. Is this someone you would like to become? Why or why not?
3. What do you need in order to allow the Big Girl inside you to come out?
4. Do you think it's possible? If so, why? If not, why not?

Group Discussion

1. How did you define a Big Girl when you were a little girl?
2. What is good about being a Big Girl?
3. What do you believe to be some of the challenges of growing up into a mature woman?

CHAPTER ONE: GOD'S HEART FOR HIS GIRLS

Personal Reflection

1. Have you accepted that God was purposeful in placing you in your family? If yes, how does this affect your view of becoming a Big Girl? If not, what could help you make peace with this idea?
2. Do you have any clues about His plans for you? Write down your thoughts.
3. Have you taken any detours from God's plan for you (as far as you know His plan today)?
4. Has God brought you back around? How? If not, do you want Him to bring you back to His plan?

Group Discussion

1. Throughout the process of growing up, God is always with us, gently nudging us with compassion and help until we can "get it" for ourselves. When have you felt God's "nudges" in your life? Describe what they have been like.
2. How have you responded to these nudges in the past? How do you hope to respond in the future?
3. Pick out your favorite part of Psalm 139:13–18. What is God saying about you in this passage?

Chapter Two:
Are You a Big Girl or a Little Girl?

Personal Reflection

1. What are some of the issues of the Little Girl? How do you feel about them personally?

2. Do you really want to choose the path to maturity? Why or why not? If not, what would it take to convince you to choose it?

Group Discussion

1. How do you think Little-Girl issues interfere with God's plans?

2. As you understand them now, describe the three most significant characteristics of the Big Girl.

3. Describe what is most appealing to you about becoming a Big Girl.

4. How would you explain to someone else how to become a Big Girl?

5. This chapter discusses how Hannah Whitall Smith chose to live in what she called "the optimism of grace." What does this optimism have to do with the Big-Girl life?

Chapter Three: How a Big Girl Speaks, How a Big Girl Thinks

Personal Reflection

1. What Little-Girl choices have you made that have caused you grief? (You can use "code" so only you will know what you are talking about in case someone picks up your book.)

2. On a scale of 1 to 10 (1 being Little Girlish and 10 being Big Girlish), how would you rate your speech?

3. What are you willing to do to let God work in that area of your life?

4. How do you view the way that you think? If you could change one thing about your thinking (and you can) what would it be?

5. What was the last thing in which you rejoiced? How long has it been?

6. List at least three things God has changed in you. Thank Him for His work in you!

Group Discussion

1. What do we hear in our speech that tips us off to Little-Girl patterns? Big-Girl patterns?

2. What are some Little-Girl ways we would like for God to take out of us?

3. Who would be willing to share at least one thing God has changed in your life to help you change from a Little Girl to a Big Girl? (Look for a volunteer.)

CHAPTER FOUR:
CONFIDENCE FOR BIG-GIRL SINGLES

Personal Reflection

1. In your own words, what do you think is the core issue that we all face as females?

2. Write out some of the Big-Girl ways in which you are embracing your singleness. How can this list help you to stay focused on God's plans for you in this season of life?

3. What is your biggest challenge as a single? How does writing it down and examining it for what it is affect your perception of it?

Group Discussion

1. Does the issue of singleness affect you right now? If yes, how? If not, why?
2. Whether you are single or not, have you ever encountered codependency in a relationship? How has it affected you? What can we invite Christ to do in our lives today to overcome codependency?
3. If you're not single now, what can you do to prepare yourself for the possibility of being single someday? After all, most of us will be single at some point in our lives.

CHAPTER FIVE:
WISDOM FOR BIG-GIRL WIVES

Personal Reflection

1. Are you experiencing pressures in your marriage? If so (use your code) what is causing it? What have you done about it?
2. Is your marriage a two-adult arrangement, or are you struggling with some immaturity on either side?
3. What is the best aspect of your marriage? How can this aspect inspire you toward an even stronger, closer relationship?
4. Do you see some of the characteristics of a Big-Girl wife in you? If so, what are they? If you see several Little-Girl traits, what would you like to do about them?

Group Discussion

1. Can we see ourselves as OK, regardless of whether we have perfect marriages or not? If not, what often stands in the way of our self-acceptance? What might change this?
2. What does a healthy view of submission mean to you?
3. What words best describe a Big-Girl wife to you? What steps can we take today to begin moving more in that direction?

Chapter Six: Savvy for Big-Girl Moms

Personal Reflection

1. Are personal principles part of your parenting style? If yes, what are some of those principles? If not, what would you like them to be?
2. Can you verbalize your boundaries? Are they what you want them to be? If not, how would you change them?
3. How would you define your authority as a Big-Girl mom?
4. Have you had to "let go" of your child or children? What has it been like for you?

Group Discussion

1. What are some differences you see between a Big-Girl mom and a Little-Girl mom?
2. Who would be willing to describe your disciplinary style? Does it work for you? In what ways do you think you could improve what you are currently doing?
3. Every season of parenting is different. Where are some of you now, and what is most important to you in this season? How can you stay focused on the priorities it requires of you?

4. List some ways that various ones of you have been a blessing to your children.

5. If you could change anything about your role as a parent, what would it be? When and how do you think you could do it? Whom can you enlist for help and support?

CHAPTER SEVEN:
FREEDOM FOR BIG-GIRL FRIENDS

Personal Reflection

1. List some mistakes you think you have made in friendship.

2. Have you ever been betrayed by a friend? How did that make you feel?

3. What do you require of your friends? What do they require of you? Are these healthy, Big-Girl requirements? Why or why not?

4. What differences between you and your friends bother you? What differences draw you closer together?

5. List your three closest friends and name the qualities you love the most in each one. Are these Big-Girl traits?

6. What would you like to do in order to be a better friend?

Group Discussion

1. What are some wonderful things you have learned through your Big-Girl friendships?

2. What are some phrases that must always be avoided between friends? Why?

3. What are some healing words that can make any relationship stronger?

4. What do you think healthy accountability looks like in a friendship? Have you ever experienced it? How well did it work?

CHAPTER EIGHT:
COURAGE FOR BIG GIRLS FACING CONFLICT

Personal Reflection

1. How do you handle conflict? Do you recognize yourself in any of the "how not to handle conflict" points listed in this chapter?
2. Describe the way you listen. Is it effective? Why or why not?
3. Have you ever asked God to search you? What could the value of such a request be?
4. What are your biggest fears about creating a crisis? Can you see the value of such a plan?
5. What are you personally willing to do in order to bring a conflict to an end?

Group Discussion

1. How could we apply the principle of the "divided baby" to any conflict we may have? How could this principle change the way we react?
2. How can we know when God is giving us wisdom?
3. What can we expect from God when we ask Him to do something?
4. Will a conflict typically "resolve itself"? If so, how? If not, why not?

CHAPTER NINE:
STABILITY FOR BIG GIRLS IN CRISIS

Personal Reflection

1. For your own personal understanding, how would you describe your crisis management style?
2. What have you learned from handling a crisis that you want to remember for the next time around?
3. What "baggage" do you need to identify and deal with in your life? (You might want to use your code here, if your "baggage" is a loved one who might read your notebook.)
4. Name at least one good thing that has come from your latest crisis. How does naming the good side of crises affect your perspective of life's trials?

Group Discussion

1. Who has ever faced a crisis? Who would be willing to tell us about your crisis?
2. Do you like the way you handled it? What do you wish you had done differently?
3. What things can we name that have gotten us through crises in the past? What are some truths that we can cling to?
4. What would you add to the list of things Big Girls need to know to stand by people in times of crisis?

CHAPTER TEN:
LEAVING A GODLY LEGACY

Personal Reflection

1. Write out a Big-Girl philosophy for yourself. Include a personal definition of what it means to be a Big Girl and a description of the value you expect to find in pursuing maturity.

2. Make a list of the Big Girls who are leaving you a legacy. What do you value about these women?

3. Name a couple of Big Girls in process with whom you would like to have a relationship. What is your plan for getting to know them better?

4. God is crazy about you and has great plans for your life! Write Him a love letter from His Big Girl. Tell Him how much you love Him and how excited you are to anticipate the fulfillment of His plans.

Group Discussion

1. Who are some of the Big Girls that have influenced you in a positive way?

2. What treasures would we like to pass on to the Big Girls in process who are following us? What do we want them to remember about us?

3. How can we begin to pass on these treasures?

4. What readings have positively impacted your life and walk with the Lord? Who is your favorite Big-Girl author?

ABOUT THE AUTHOR

 JAN SILVIOUS is an author, counselor, and popular speaker who believes that women do best when they are free to be who God created them to be. Described as the female "Dr. Phil," Jan is a no-nonsense speaker who captivates and motivates her audience. She is the author of several books including *The Five Minute Devotional, Foolproofing Your Life,* and *Look at it This Way.* Jan is currently speaking her Big Girl message at the 2004 Women of Faith conferences across the country. She and her husband, Charlie, live in Chattanooga, TN not far from their three grown sons, two wonderful daughters-in-law, and five grandchildren.

EXTRAORDINARY*faith*

CONFERENCE *2005*

2005 EVENT CITIES & SPECIAL GUESTS

NATIONAL CONFERENCE **LAS VEGAS, NV** FEBRUARY 17-19 Thomas & Mack Center	**KANSAS CITY, MO** JUNE 3-4 Kemper Arena *Natalie Grant, Chonda Pierce, Jennifer Rothschild*	**SACRAMENTO, CA** AUGUST 5-6 ARCO Arena *Avalon, Kristin Chenoweth, Tammy Trent*	**HARTFORD, CT** SEPT. 30 – OCT. 1 Hartford Civic Center *Sandi Patty, Chonda Pierce, Tammy Trent*
NATIONAL CONFERENCE **FT. LAUDERDALE, FL** FEBRUARY 24-26 Office Depot Center	**ST. LOUIS, MO** JUNE 17-18 Savvis Center *Avalon, Nichole Nordeman, Chonda Pierce*	**PORTLAND, OR** AUGUST 12-13 Rose Garden Arena *Kristin Chenoweth, Natalie Grant, Tammy Trent*	**SEATTLE, WA** OCTOBER 7-8 Key Arena *Sandi Patty, Chonda Pierce, Jennifer Rothschild*
SHREVEPORT, LA APRIL 1-2 CenturyTel Center *Sandi Patty, Chonda Pierce, Jennifer Rothschild*	**CANADA & NEW ENGLAND CRUISE** JUNE 25 – JULY 2 *Tammy Trent*	**DENVER, CO** AUGUST 19-20 Pepsi Center *Avalon, Kristin Chenoweth, Nichole Nordeman*	**DES MOINES, IA** OCTOBER 14-15 Wells Fargo Arena *Sandi Patty, Chonda Pierce, Jennifer Rothschild*
HOUSTON, TX APRIL 8-9 Toyota Center *Kristin Chenoweth, Natalie Grant, Jennifer Rothschild*	**ATLANTA, GA** JULY 8-9 Philips Arena *Natalie Grant, Sherri Shepherd, Tammy Trent*	**DALLAS, TX** AUGUST 26-27 American Airlines Center *Avalon, Kristin Chenoweth, Nichole Nordeman*	**ST. PAUL, MN** OCTOBER 21-22 Xcel Energy Center *Sandi Patty, Chonda Pierce, Jennifer Rothschild*
COLUMBUS, OH APRIL 15-16 Nationwide Arena *Avalon, Kristin Chenoweth, Nichole Nordeman*	**FT. WAYNE, IN** JULY 15-16 Allen County War Memorial Coliseum *Sandi Patty, Chonda Pierce, Jennifer Rothschild*	**ANAHEIM, CA** SEPTEMBER 9-10 Arrowhead Pond *Avalon, Chonda Pierce, Tammy Trent*	**CHARLOTTE, NC** OCTOBER 28-29 Charlotte Coliseum *Sandi Patty, Beth Moore, Sherri Shepherd*
BILLINGS, MT MAY 13-14 MetraPark *Sandi Patty, Chonda Pierce, Jennifer Rothschild*	**DETROIT, MI** JULY 22-23 Palace of Auburn Hills *Sherri Shepherd, Tammy Trent, CeCe Winans*	**PHILADELPHIA, PA** SEPTEMBER 16-17 Wachovia Center *Kathie Lee Gifford, Natalie Grant, Nichole Nordeman*	**OKLAHOMA CITY, OK** NOVEMBER 4-5 Ford Center *Kristin Chenoweth, Sandi Patty, Chonda Pierce*
PITTSBURGH, PA MAY 20-21 Mellon Arena *Natalie Grant, Nichole Nordeman, Chonda Pierce*	**WASHINGTON, DC** JULY 29-30 MCI Center *Natalie Grant, Nichole Nordeman, Sherri Shepherd*	**ALBANY, NY** SEPTEMBER 23-24 Pepsi Arena *Sandi Patty, Chonda Pierce*	**ORLANDO, FL** NOVEMBER 11-12 TD Waterhouse Centre *Avalon, Chonda Pierce, Tammy Trent*

1-888-49-FAITH womenoffaith.com

Guests subject to change. Not all guests appear in every city. Visit womenoffaith.com for details on special guests, registration deadlines and pricing.